"Disasters, Religion, Wars, and Celestial Physics"

Disclaimer

46 St. Books
Published by 46 St. Books
46 St. Books USA Inc.,
Philadelphia, PA 19144, USA

Copyright © William C. Henry Sr., 2014

All rights reserved under International and Pan-American Copyright Conventions.

ISBN 13# – 978-0-9916520-1-3   ISBN 10# - 0991652010

Library of Congress Cataloging-in-Publication Data

LCCN#

Henry Sr., William.
Disasters, Religion, Wars, and Celestial Physics

PRINTED IN THE UNITED STATES OF AMERICA

PUBLISHER'S NOTE
This book is a work of non-fictional based on archival scriptures, texts, and documents. All images used are either owned, work for hire, acquired works, use with permission, and from the Library of Congress.

BOOKS ARE AVAILABLE AT QUANTITY DISCOUNTS WHEN USED TO PROMOTE PRODUCTS OR SERVICES. FOR INFORMATION PLEASE WRITE 46 ST. BOOKS, 55 WEST PENN ST, PHILADELPHIA, PA 19144 OR VISIT OUR WEBSITE AT WWW.46STBOOKS.COM

Table of Content

Dedication   - pg 7

The Solar Harmonic Battery   - pg 9

Geometry of the Universe   - pg 11

432 or 440: Heavenly or Harmful Frequency   - pg13

432 The Universal Frequency   - pg17

The Broken Egg and Plate Tectonics   - pg 23

360° to 330° Portion of the Heavens 1/12th - Scorpio Age   - pg 33

330° to 300° Portion of the Heavens 2/12th - Libra Age   - pg 35

300° to 270° Portion of the Heavens 3/12th - Virgo Age   - pg 37

270° to 240° Portion of the Heavens 4/12th - Leo Age   - pg 39

240° to 210° Portion of the Heavens 5/12th - Cancer Age   - pg 43

210° to 180° Portion of the Heavens 6/12th - Gemini Age   - pg 47

180° to 150° Portion of the Heavens 7/12th - Taurus Age   - pg 51

150° to 120° Portion of the Heavens 8/12th - Aries Age   - pg 57

120° to 90° Portion of the Heavens 9/12th - Pisces Age   - pg 73

90° to 60° Portion of the Heavens 10/12th - Aquarius Age   - pg 93

60° to 30° Portion of the Heavens 11/12th - Capricorn Age   - pg 95

30° to 360° Portion of the Heavens 12/12th - Sagittarius Age   - pg 96

Conclusions   - pg 97

Various Graphs   - pg 99

Disasters Pauses Warfare! - pg 101

Major Volcanic Events and Solar Minimums and Maximums   - pg 105

The Birth of Venus and Kiloyear Events   - pg 107

Dedication

    I dedicate this book to my sons William Jr. and Justin. I am fortunate to have you as sons, and my desire is for you to always hunger for knowledge, and that you never allow your soul and mind to be dictated by another's delusions. Always base your knowledge on a basis of true understanding, and not one of superstition that traumatizes ones spirit. Enjoy this wonderful transition that we find ourselves in, find the beauty in that which is others find ugly and unworthy. Adore the light while embracing the dark, as there are areas of grey that must be experienced for growth. You may see our world as an insane existence, but it is of our doing that we find it so. Inject love, understanding, tolerance, and friendship to one and all, just as my love and support is always yours for always!

Thank you Tengam

AHTYT!

The Solar Harmonic Battery

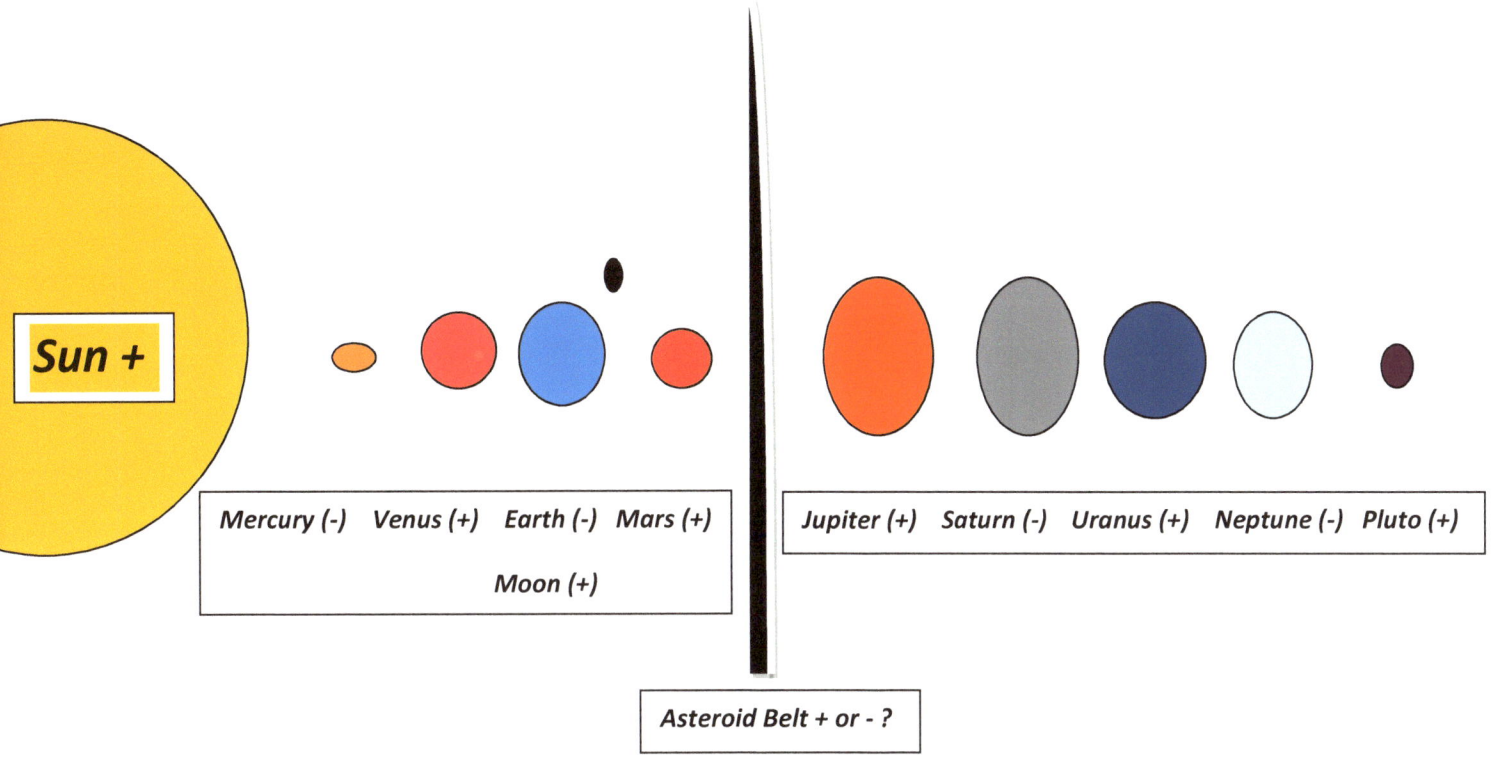

    When I look at the celestial alignment that is our solar system, I am constantly awestruck with the beautiful complexity and simplicity of the design. There is a dance that has been going on for billions of years led by an excellent bandmaster. The Sun is the one that sets the pace and tempo for all of the planets, exerting the needed force to keep all of the dancers in step. The solar system is set up in an attractive format. I say attractive, as opposites attract.

    The polarity of each planet having either a negative (-) or positive (+) polarity determines the placement of that celestial sphere. If any of these spheres were to slip from the celestial bar, then the rule of attractions would apply. A negative and positive charge would attract, just as two alike polarities would repel one another. The reason that we have a tidal lock with the Moon is due to the Moon having a negative polarity. Every planet is basically a battery that is negatively or positively charged!

Geometry of the Universe

    The physical setup of the Universe shows all of the classical understanding of Pythagoras. The Greek Mystery schools sprang forth from the knowledge brought back from Egypt and Babylon, whose Mystery schools were in operation several thousand years prior. Pythagoras saved for us the beautiful understanding of how geometry interplays with shapes and frequency. The 360°s of the sky has been laid out in a precise and exacting order to regulate our existence.

2 Dimensional Shapes

Shape	Degree Sum	Math	Music Note
Triangle	180°	180 ÷ 3 = 60°	F#
Circle	360°	360 = completion	F#
Square	360°	360 ÷ 4 = 90°	F#
Pentagon	540°	540 ÷ 5 = 120°	C#
Hexagon	720°	720 ÷ 6 = 120°	F#
Heptagon	900°	*900 ÷ 7sides = 128.571°	A#
Octagon	1080°	1080 ÷ 8 sides = 135°	C#
Nonagon	1260°	1260 ÷ 9 = 1240°	

3 part major cord F#

*The heptagon is the only 2D shape in the group that breaks down to a fraction!

3 Dimensional Shapes

Shape	Platonic Solid	Degree Sum	Math	Music Note
Tetrahedron	Fire	720°	720 ÷ 8 = 90	F#
Octahedron	Air	1440°	1440 ÷ 8 = 180	F# High
Cube/Hexahedron	Earth	2160°	2160 ÷ 6 = 360	C# High
Icosahedron	Water	3600°	*N/A	A#
Dodecahedron	Ether	3600°	*N/A	A#

432 or 440 - Heavenly or Harmful Frequency?

Musical Note	432 Diatonic G Scale Factor 9	440 Musical Scale	Musical Note	432 or 440? Listed Below	Solfeggio Frequency	Electrical Frequency
	9			432	63	
	18				174	147
	27				285	294
D	36	27.500	A0	432	396	348
F#	45	29.135			417	441
A	54	30.868	B0		528	588
C	63	32.703	C1		639	696
D	72	34.648		432	741	735
E	81	36.708	D1		852	870
F#	90	38.891		432	963	942
G#	99	41.203	E1		1074	1056
A	108	43.654	F1	432	1185	1188
B	117	46.249			1296	1251
C	126	48.999	G1	432	1317	1323
C#	135	51.913			1428	1413
D	144	55.000	A1	432	1539	1566
D#	153	58.270-			1641	1668
E	162	61.735	B1	432	1752	1764
F	171	65.406	C2		1863	1845
F#	180	69.269		432	1974	1980
G	189	73.416	D2		2085	1058
G#	198	77.782			2196	2142
Ab	207	82.407	E2		2217	2214
A	216	87.307	F2	432	2328	2352
A#	225	92.499			2439	2436
B	234	97.999	G2		2541	2580
	243				2652	2640
C	252	103.83		432	2763	2772
	261				2874	2889
C#	270	110.00-	A2	432	2985	2964
	279				3096	3096
D	288	116.34		432	3117	3135
	297				3228	3297
D#	306	123.47	B2	432	3339	3336
	315				3441	3420
E	324	130.81	C3	432	3552	3564
F	342	138.59			3663	3690
F#	360	146.83	D3	432	3774	3768
G	378	155.36			3885	3870

G#	*396*	164.81	E3	*432*	3996	3990
Ab	414	174.61	F3		4017	4059
A	432	185.00-		*432*	4128	4128
A#	450	196.00-	G3		4239	4239
B	456	207.65			4341	4356
C	504	220.00-	A3	*432*	4452	4446
C#	540	233.08		*432*	4563	4560
D	576	246.94	B3	*432*	4674	4680
D#	612	261.63	C4*		4785	4797
E	648	277.18		*432*	4896	4851
F	684	293.66	D4		4917	4950
F#	720	311.13		*432*	5028	5004
G	756	329.83	E4		5139	5148
G#	792	349.23	F4	*432*	5241	5238
Ab	828	369.99			5352	5280
A	864	392.00-	G4	*432*	5463	5421
A#	900	415.30-		*432*	5574	5535
B	*936*	440.00-	A4*	*432 / 440*	5685	5652
C	1008	466.16		*432*	5796	5778
C#	1080	493.88	B4	*432*	5817	5808
D	1152	523.55	C5	*432*	5928	5940
D#	1224	554.37			6039	5964
E	1296	587.33	D5	*432*	6141	6123
F	1368	622.23			6252	6255
F#	1440	659.28	E5	*432*	6363	6390
G	1512	698.46	F5		6474	6426
G#	1584	739.99			6585	6594
Ab	1656	783.99	G5		6696	6669
A	1728	830.81		*432*	6717	6741
A#	1800	880.00-	A5		6828	6816
B	1872	932.33			6939	6930
C	2016	987.77	B5		7041	7029
C#	2160	1046.5	C6	*432*	7152	7140
D	2304	1108.7		*432*	7263	7392
D#	2448	1174.7	D6		7374	7410
E	2592	1244.5		*432*	7485	7488
F	2736	1318.5	E6		7596	7566
F#	2880	1396.9	F6		7617	7623
G	3024	1480.00-			7728	7704
G#	3168	1568.0-	G6		7839	7854
Ab	3312	1661.2			7941	7920
A	3456	1760.0-	A6		8052	8148
A#	3600	1864.7		*432*	8163	8151
B	3755	1975.5	B6		8274	8250
C	4032	2093.0-	C7		8385	8316
C#	4320	2217.5-			8496	8424

D	4608	2349.3	D7		8517	8568
D#	4896	2489			8628	8667
E	5184	2637.0-	E7	432	8739	8730
F	5472	2789.0-	F7		8841	8892
F#	5760	2960.0-		432	8952	8946
G	6048	3136.0-	G7		9063	9009
G#	6336	3322.4			9174	9075
Ab	6624	3520.0-	A7		9285	9282
A	6912	3729.3			9396	9360
A#	7200	3951.1	B7	432	9417	9372
B	7510	4186.0-	C8		9528	9585

The 432 Hz Scale is clearly the tonal frequency that was deemed to be, as all frequencies on the scale can be reduced to a Pythagorean 9!

432 the Universal Frequency

432 Freq.	Solar-Universal Relevancy
36	36° solar point - 3600 days = 1 Tun
72	72° solar point - 7200 days = 1 Katun
90	90° solar point
108	108° solar point Rings of Saturn - 108,000 miles in diameter
126	126 hr. week = 18 hr X 7 days (24 hr = 168 hrs) = 42 hours added to the week and 6 hours to the day to the present 24 hour day
144	144° solar point - 144,000 days = 1 Baktun
162	1620 hrs = 540 X 3
180	180° solar point - 180° triangle sum
216	216° solar point - 216 is half of 432
252	252° solar point
270	270° solar point - 540 hrs / 2 = 270 hrs.
288	288° solar point - 2,888,000 days = 1 Piktun
306	306,720,000 Solar years = 1 Maha Yuga
324	324° solar point - 540 hrs mo X 6 mos = 3240 hrs - 6480 hrs yr X 50 yr Jubilee = 324,000 hrs
360	360° solar point - 360° circle/square sum
378	540 hrs mo X 7 = 3780 hrs
396	3960 = 360 X 11 3960 miles Earth's equator to north or south poles
432	432 = 360 X 12 - 432 Magic freq - 2160/5=432 - 432 squared only # almost = to light speed 186,624 (186,282.397) - 432,000 yrs. In a Kali Yuga - 3,600 X 12 = 432,000 - 540 hrs mo X 8 = 4320 hrs 5 Miles Per Second to Miles Per Day = 432,000 50 Miles Per Second to Miles Per Day = 4,320,000 500 Miles Per Second to Miles Per Day = 43,200,000
504	5040 miles Earth's equator to Moons equator stacked atop
540	540° Pentagon sum -540 hrs mo = 18 hrs X 30 days / 540 hrs mo X 12 = 6480 hr yr / 3 = 2160 - 540 hrs mo X 10 = 5400 hrs
576	57,600 days = 1 Kalabtun
648	64,800 = 3600 secs hr X 18 hr day - 64,800 secs X 360 days = 6480 hrs - 6480 yrs = 3 Zodiac Ages - 6480 hrs X 4 = 25,920 hrs/yrs - 6480 hr /yr X 400 yrs = 2,592,000 - Earth's daily mileage
720	720° hexagon / tetrahedron sum
792	7920 miles Earth north to south pole
864	86,400 seconds 24hr. Day (86,400/2160=432) and (86,400 - 64,800 = 21,600!) - 864,000 miles Suns diameter - 864,000 Solar years = 1 Dvapara Yuga 1 Miles Per Second to Miles Per Day = 86,400 10 Miles Per Second to Miles Per Day = 864,000 100 Miles Per Second to Miles Per Day = 8,640,000
900	900° septagon sum
936	936
1008	10,080 miles south pole of Earth to north pole of the Moon stacked atop
1080	1080° octagon sum - 1080 mins = 60 mins X 18 hr day 1080 miles Moon's equator to south or north poles
1152	1,152,000,000 days = 1 Kinchitun
1296	1,296,000 Solar years (400/394.26) = 1 Treta Yuga
1440	1440° Octahedron sum - 1440 = 60 mins X 24 hrs - 144,000 days sealed Revelations - 1 Baktun = 144,000 days - 144,000 casing stones Giza pyramid

1728	1,728,000 Solar years = 1 Satya Yuga 2 Miles Per Second to Miles Per Day = 172,800 20 Miles Per Second to Miles Per Day = 1,728,000 200 Miles Per Second to Miles Per Day = 17,280,000
2160	2160° cube sum - 2160 miles Moons diameter - 21,600 = 60 mins X 360°/day/year - Ezekiel 6:3 (9) - 60 cubits X 60 cubits = 3600 cubits or 60 X 60 X 60 = 216,000 X 2 = 432,000
2304	23,040,000,000 days = 1 Alautun
2592	25,920 yrs. = 1 Zodiac Age (12 X 2160) / 6480 yrs X 4 = 25,920 yrs - 2,592,000 miles Earth daily travels - 2,592,000 hrs / 360 = 7200 hrs / 18 hrs = 400 Tropical Yrs - 259,200,000 yrs = 1 Brahma month 3 Miles Per Second to Miles Per Day = 259,200 miles 30 Miles Per Second to Miles Per Day = 2,592,000 miles 300 Miles Per Second to Miles Per Day = 25,920,000 miles
3456	4 Miles Per Second to Miles Per Day = 345,600 miles 40 Miles Per Second to Miles Per Day = 3,456,000 miles 400 Miles Per Second to Miles Per Day = 34,560,000 miles
3600	3600° icosahedron and dodecahedron sum - 3600 = 3600 X 10
5184	51,840,000 seconds / 144,000 = 360 6 Miles Per Second to Miles Per Day = 518,400 miles 60 Miles Per Second to Miles Per Day = 5,184,000 miles 600 Miles Per Second to Miles Per Day = 51,840,000 miles 6 Miles Per Second to Miles Per Day = 518,400 miles 60 Miles Per Second to Miles Per Day = 5,184,000 miles 600 Miles Per Second to Miles Per Day = 51,840,000 miles
5760	57,600,000 days = 1 Kalabtun
7200	Distance Earth to Moon = 2,592,000 miles / 360 = 7200

432 the number of Creation:

36 - On the Mayan calendar 3600 days equal 1 Tun and the 36th solar point

72 - On the Mayan calendar 7200 days equal 1 Katun

The 72nd solar point

Recent Events 72: 3/7/2014 Malaysia flight MH-370, 3/11/2004 Madrid train bombing, 3/11/2012 Fukushima earthquake, tsunami, and nuclear disaster, 3/11/2013 Boston Marathon bombing

90 - The 90th solar point

108 - The 108th solar point, and the rings of Saturn are 108,000 miles in diameter, while being thinner than a sheet of paper

126 - The 126th solar point - shows how earths original 18 hour day times 7 days equals 126 hours, an adjustment of 42 additional after disasters gives us the present 168 hour week of 24 hour days.

144 - The 144th solar point, on the Mayan calendar 144,000 days equal 1 Baktun

162 - The 162nd solar point, and 540 hours times 3 equals 1,620 hours

180 - The 180th solar point, and 180°s equals the sum of an equilateral triangle

216 - The 216th solar point, the 216 is half of the magic frequency of 432

252 - The 252nd solar point

Recent Events 252: *Pentagon foundation laid 9/11/1941, Pentagon hit by an aircraft 9/11/2001, World Trade Center Towers 1,2,6,and 7 destroyed by two aircraft on 9/11/2001, and an aircraft in Schenksville, PA is brought down on 9/11/2001*

270 - The 270th solar point, and 540 hours divided by 2 equals 270 hours

306 - The 306th solar point, and on the Hindu calendar 306,720,000 solar years equals 1 Maha Yuga

360 - The 360th solar point, and 360°s equals the sum of a circle or a square (Squaring the Circle)

378 - 540 hours times 7 equals 3,780 hours

396 - The distance from the earth's equator to the north or south poles is exactly 3,960 miles or 360 times 11 equals 3,960

432 - The only number when squared that most closely approximates the speed of light (186,624) is 432 (186,282.397)**,** when 360 is multiplied by 12 it equals 432, a zodiac age of 2,160 years divided by 5 equals 432 years, 3,600 times 12 equals 432,000, 540 hours times 8 equals 4,320 hours, and 432,000 years equals 1 Kali Yuga on the Hindu calendar, 5 Miles Per Second to Miles Per Day = 432,000 miles   50 Miles Per Second to Miles Per Day = 4,320,000 miles   500 Miles Per Second to Miles Per Day = 43,200,000 miles

504 - If you stacked the moon on top of the earth and measured the distance from the earth's equator (3,960 mi) to the moon's equator (1,080 mi) it would be 5,040 miles

540 - The sum of a pentagon is 540°s, an 18 hour day times 30 days equals 540 hours per month - times 12 months equals 6,480 hours per year - divided by 3 equals 2,160, and 10 times 540 hours equals 5400 hours

576 - On the Mayan calendar 57,600 days equal 1 Kalabtun

648 - An 18 hour day times 3600 seconds per hour equals 64,800 seconds per day - times 360 days equals 23,328,000 seconds or 6,480 hours, 6,480 years equals 3 zodiac ages (2,160 yrs) times 4 equals 25,920 years or 1 complete zodiac cycle - that same 25,920 miles time times 100 equals 2,592,000 miles or the distance in miles that the earth travels daily

720 - The sum of a hexagon is 720°s, and the sum of a platonic solid the tetrahedron is 720°s

792 - The distance from the north pole to the south pole is exactly 7,920 miles

864 - There are 86,400 seconds in a 24 hour day as 86,400 divided by 2,160 equals 432 - 86,400 minus 64,800 equals the post disaster increase of 21,600 annual seconds, on the Hindu calendar 864,000 solar years equals 1 Dvarapa Yuga, and the Sun is 864,000 miles in diameter, 1 Miles Per Second to Miles Per

Day = 86,400 miles   10 Miles Per Second to Miles Per Day = 864,000 miles   100 Miles Per Second to Miles Per Day = 8,640,000 miles

900 - The sum of a septagon is 900°s

936 - A Golden Number

1008 - If you stacked the moon on top of the earth it would be 10,080 miles from the south pole of earth to the north pole of the moon

1080 - The sum of an octagon is 1080°s, the distance from the moon's equator to south or north pole is 1,080 miles, and an 18 hour day times 60 minutes equals 1080 minutes per day

1152 - On the Mayan calendar 1 Kinchitun equals 1,152,000,000 days

1296 - On the Hindu calendar 1 Treta Yuga equals 1,296,000 solar years

1440 - The sum of an octahedron is 1440°s, the adjusted 24 hour day times 60 minutes equals 1,440 minutes per day, there will be 144,000 sealed in the Christian Book of Revelations verse 7:4, the Great Pyramid of Giza was originally lined with 144,000 exterior casing stones (1 Solar Year), and on the Mayan calendar 144,000 days equals 1 Baktun

1728 - On the Hindu calendar 1,728,000 solar years equals 1 Satya Yuga, 2 Miles Per Second to Miles Per Day = 172,800 miles   20 Miles Per Second to Miles Per Day = 1,728,000 miles   200 Miles Per Second to Miles Per Day = 17,280,000 miles

2160 - The sum of a cubes/hexahedron angles is 2,160°s as the cube is venerated in the Jewish and Islamic faith, the diameter of the moon is 2,160 miles, if we multiply 60 times 360 days/degrees/years equals 21,600, as Ezekiel 6:3 in the Christian Bible relates the building of the 2nd Temple should be 60 X 60 X 60 cubits or 216,000 cubits, and 216,000 times 2 equals 432,000 or 1 Kali Yuga

2304 - On the Mayan calendar 23,040,000,000 days equal 1 Alautun

2592 - A complete zodiac cycle is 25,920 years divided by 12 equals 2,160 years per zodiac age, 2,592 times 1,000 equals 2,592,000 years or the distance of the earth to the moon, 2,592,000 divided by 360 equals 7200 - times 18 hours equals 400 solar years, and on the Hindu calendar 259,200,000 years equals 1 Brahma month, 3 Miles Per Second to Miles Per Day = 259,200 miles   30 Miles Per Second to Miles Per Day = 2,592,000 miles   300 Miles Per Second to Miles Per Day = 25,920,000 miles

3456 - 4 Miles Per Second to Miles Per Day = 345,600 miles   40 Miles Per Second to Miles Per Day = 3,456,000 miles   400 Miles Per Second to Miles Per Day = 34,560,000 miles

3600 - The sum of an icosahedron is 3600°s, the sum of a dodecahedron is 3600°s,

5184 - When we take 51,840,000 seconds divided by 144,000 equals 360, 6 Miles Per Second to Miles Per Day = 518,400 miles   60 Miles Per Second to Miles Per Day = 5,184,000 miles   600 Miles Per Second to Miles Per Day = 51,840,000 miles

5760 - *On the Mayan calendar 1 Kalabtun is equal to 57,600,000*

7200 - *When 7200 is multiplied by 360 it equals 2,592,000 or the distance of the earth to the moon*

The Broken Egg and Plate Tectonics

I will cut straight to the heart of the matter, as the earth was a one continent/Pangean land mass as recently as 2344 BCE! All the evidence points to plate tectonics as being a very recent phenomenon in regard to natural planetary processes. The theory of plate tectonics was put forth in the 1950's based on earlier concepts. I will layout below a clear picture of how plate tectonics came about, and the disasters that brought this current land formation into being.

The word tectonic comes from the Greek "tectonicus," meaning pertaining to building. This scientific theory has been accepted as to how the earth's lithosphere functions in regard to large scale motion. This model builds its platform on the concept of continental drift which came about during the early portion of the 20th century. The scientific community accepted the theory in conjunction with the spreading sea floor theory developed in the 1950s to 1960's.

The lithosphere is the outermost shell of the planet, as it is broken into eight major plates and many minor plates. The intersection of these plates are called convergent, divergent, or transform plates. Earthquakes, volcanic activity, mountain building, and oceanic trench formation occurs along these plates. Plate movement is thought to be caused by the spreading of the seafloor away from the ridge. Global rotation, along with the influence of the Sun and Moon have been attributed as aiding in the process.

Professor Charles Hapgood, put forth the "Earth-Crust Displacement" theory that was not met warmly in the academic community. The theory held that due to pole shifts, the earth's crust could slide as a separate layer bringing disaster. Meteorologist Alfred Wegener described in 1912 what he called "continental drift," of which he expanded on in 1915 with his book "The Origins of Continents and Oceans." The starting idea was that the present continents started from one land mass later called Pangea that slowly drifted apart. Later support came in for this theory based on the outlines of Africa and South America. Paleomagnetism was used to support this platform, as rocks of differing ages show a variable magnetic field direction. Based on the current model plate tectonics started around 3 billion years ago, as the continents spread further apart at the rate of 1.5 inches annually.

The problem with plate tectonics and continental drift, is that they are theories that are almost impossible to prove or disprove as scientifically accurate. I feel very strongly that I have solved that puzzle in large part. When we look at the other terrestrial planets there is a notable lack of continents. Venus has two highland continents Ishtar Terra and Aphrodite Terra. Mars has a single land mass (two highlands) with several areas noted as Arabia Terra, Amazonia Plantia, Planum Boreum, and Planum Australe, as well as two polar caps. Mercury has two distinct plains with no known tectonic activity. We are the only planet with continents and tectonic activity, which shows there was some sort of external or internal influence in the creation of these processes.

The earth held one land mass in 2344 BCE, and the inflation from one continent to seven separate pieces occurred in an instant versus 3 billion years. Rocks do not slowly break apart over time!

When we look at features such as the Sifra Ridge, the ridge shows jagged rupturing of the rock mass on massive scale. The whole of the basis for plate tectonics was built upon the also flawed continental drift theory. The force that would cause one cohesive landmass to slowly separate has never been fully explained? All things being equal the force would have to be phenomenal. When you think of massive influences, we have to look externally and internally. I believe that there was an internal action brought about by external forces that ripped one continent into seven overnight.

"External Force"

The external force that played into this process had to be either an asteroid, comet, or planet. I feel confident that neither asteroids nor comets aided in this particular destruction of our biosphere. The object that assumed a periodic parabolic trajectory around the earth had to be a planet of influential size and mass. The lithosphere is up to 62 miles thick. The planet that brought this disaster about as an external influence was none other than Venus. The current place that Venus holds in the celestial bar is not always the one that she held. These theories have been put forth previously by Immanuel Velikovsky and many others.

Venus presently sits in the 2nd position from the Sun, but ancient lore holds that she was born of Jupiter. This theory was passed off by modern science, but modern science has also just witnessed Saturn giving birth to a new moon or moonlet in 2014. Professor Velikovsky posited that Venus would be hot being a young planet, would be rich in petroleum gases and hydrocarbons, and that Venus would have an abnormal orbit. All of these observations were shown to be accurate through scientific rigors. There is no seismic data available for Venus or known plate tectonics, she has a tight circular orbit with an 0.01° of eccentricity, rotates counterclockwise, the Sun rises in the West and sets in the East, and is able to transit the Sun. Velikovsky also put forth that Jupiter would emit radio noise, that the earth's magnetosphere reaches to the Moon, and that the rotation of earth can be affected by electromagnetic fields. All have been shown to be accurate!

Earth has a negative polarity while Venus has a positive polarity, which would cause two unlike bodies to be attracted to each other. Assuming that Venus took periodic approaches to earth, at some point the parabola would allow the two charged planets to interact electrically. The constituents of the two bodies would be exchanged as far as atmospheric gases. The earth is comprised primarily of N_2, O_2, Argon, and CO_2, while the atmosphere of Venus is comprised largely of CO_2, Nitrogen, and Sulfur Dioxide. How these particles would interact on a planetary scale coupled with a kick start through electrical arcing can only be speculated at this point. These normally calm particles may behave totally different on a planetary exchange scale, but the sulfur dioxide will be an issue that I will show later through related disasters. I establish Venus as the external force that helped to crack the egg that is our planet.

"Internal Force"

The external force is a bit easier to reconcile immediately, versus the internal force that was secondary to the initiation by the external force. It has puzzled me since childhood why the continents appeared to look like a puzzle piece themselves? It seemed that one need only piece the western side of

South America back to Africa on the eastern side, curl North America over to Africa, clip Madagascar back on Southern Africa, Australia to New Zealand, and Antarctica back to the southern portion of Africa, and we would have the bulk of the Pangean continent back together. I am pretty certain that many people have pondered this same enigma many a night to no avail. What mechanism on the planet would interact on that large a scale to bring this about is what I pondered. That force finally revealed itself through inspection of an anomaly in Africa.

Oklo, Gabon sits on the east coast of Africa at the equator, and a strange anomaly is found there. A natural nuclear reactor resides in Oklo, that contains a uranium deposit from a runaway chain reaction. French physicist Francis Perrin discovered in 1972 through examination of the isotope data that the U-235 had been depleted. This was dated to have happened some 1.7 billion years ago, based on the known rate of decay. Paul Kuzuo Kuroda predicted in 1956 the possibility of a natural uranium reactor whereby the layering of nuclear reactor zones, sandstone, a uranium ore layer, and granite, would exist as a natural reactor. Oklo happens to be the only known site where this was in place by nature of the 16 known sites. Normal U-235 concentration is around 0.7202% and the Oklo samples were 0.600% a significant difference. The required explanation gave the dating billions of years ago versus thousands of years.

Oklo is 85% rain forest, and consists of a coastal plain, mountain region, and a savanna. The Natal region of Brazil on the South American east coast sits at 5°'s below the equator, and has a rain forest with black sand beaches as well. The 5°s separation of Natal and Oklo shows again the 5°'s of axial rotation added to the earth by the 2344 BCE disaster event. The recent indigenous inhabitants of Gabon were the Pygmy people, and their tribes are spread over several African countries all located near the equator.

Uranium is a pyrophoric solid which when exposed to air or water may result in a nuclear reaction. On that day in 2344 BCE when Biblically one could still walk from sea to sea on one continent, the fall of Eden occurred as the egg was cracked. The one continent land mass was pulled with massive gravitational force exerted against the planet at the equators. Egypt is considered the navel of the planet and sits not far from the equator. The force of the two charged bodies ruptures the sealed natural reactor, causing either water or air, or both to rush into the mine. Once the reaction started, the runaway effect caused an explosive separation of the continent into seven main chunks. The Global Flood of record would have infused water to the earth on a scale that would have aided this reaction. The Evil Wind swirled around the planet leaving death in its wake.

I say Evil Wind as Hindu, Babylonian, Mayan, and even Biblical lore speak of an Evil Wind, Hurricane Wind, or Overthrow Wind. This Evil Wind is what led to the downfall of the Indus Valley civilization and the five cities of Megrah, Lothal, Harrapa, and Mohenjo-Dharo. The city of Mohenjo-Dharo is translated as "Mound of the Dead," and skeletons exhumed showed massive levels of radioactivity. Hindu legends tell of nuclear-like wars in the skies with tales like "The Bhagavad Gita," and this is where the epics found their basis in large part.

Since the detonation of over 2,500 nuclear weapons by humanity, our ability to accurately carbon date items has been compromised. This being the case, dates will always be open to dispute using those methods, but true understanding will always trump that platform. Disasters that transpired due to the periodic events helped to shape the world that we exist in today.

The possible birth of Venus around 13,000 BCE brings an end to the Older Dryas stadial cold period. From 12,670 BCE to 1200 BCE we experience a warm period that remained stable from 9,200 to 2,500 years ago with a pronounced cooling from 2,500 to 500 years ago, and the present high rate is unusual and is known as the Bolling-Allerod Oscillation. The Pleistocene epoch began over 2,888,000 years prior, and comes to an end in 11,700 BCE with the start of the Holocene epoch, which is the period that we currently live in. In 11,700 BCE to 10,800 BCE we get the Allerod Oscillation warm period at the onset of the Holocene. In 11,000 BCE we have a northern latitude planetary passover as ice core meltwater pulse 1A sees sea levels rise 65.7 feet. We see the first signs of warfare in 11,000 BCE, as well as a massive sudden extinction of megafauna, woolly mammoth, mastodons, and more . We get a possible Younger Dryas impact event in 10,900 BCE with the onset of a cold period.

The 10,800 BCE the West Belukha Plateau tritium reference horizon with significant sulfate peaks shows a coincidences with volcanic eruptions, and shows that the Atlai Glacier did not exist during the Bolling-Allerod, and this indicates that the air temperature was around 6.1°s cooler during the Younger Dryas. In 10,640 BCE the Grigorieva Ice Cap coincides with the beginning of the Younger Dryas cold period, as the ice cap did not exist in the Bolling-Allerod warm period which was significantly warmer than today. The global magnetic field (magnetic difference) sits at ≥8 in 10,000 BCE, as the increase in the field level increases with the external influence. Mysteriously in 10,000 BCE as well the world sea levels rises abruptly with major floods, as this correspondence shows how the external influence begins to factor in, as this change in global climate in 10,000 BCE causes the onset of the Neolithic culture.

In 9850 BCE the Wisconsin glaciation advances & retreats as shown through radiocarbon dating. As we see in 9700 BCE Lake Agassiz reforms from glacial melt-water, Long Island becomes an island, and the Bering Sea cuts off the North American path. All of these events show a clear lack of human footprints from CO2 emissions, and the volcanoes and earthquakes have yet to begin in earnest. The 9700 BCE ice records shows unusually high temperatures in the northern latitudes from 7000 BCE to 4000 BCE. We see these wild fluctuations and disasters have transpired without the infusion of carbon emissions and other modern pollutants. I am wholeheartedly in advance of planet stewardship, but we must operate from a basis of truth, and not one of hidden selfish agendas.

In 9650 BCE we begin to see renewed volcanic activity after millions of years missing from the records, with the eruption of Mount Tongariro, in 9460 BCE Taupo Volcano erupts, and in 9450 BCE Mount Tongariro erupts again, as both of these volcanoes are located in New Zealand (blew away from Australia? The volcanic activity will only increase over time, and we have yet to find our first documented earthquake. One would think that if the tectonic plates were already separated, that we would see earthquakes in the recent record, and not just millions of years in the past.

In 9500 BCE Ancylus Lake in the Baltic forms, as long-term melting of the Antarctic ice sheet begins. Yet again there is no known human cause to this onset of this melting suggestive of an external influence. Our planet is influenced by the Sun, other planets, and stars through electromagnetism, as it is not farfetched to see a disturbance in the local neighborhood. In 9500 BCE we have Plato's sinking of Atlantis (historical?) which coincides with our known scientific findings from that era! In 9270 BCE Greenland sees an abrupt and rapid rise in temperature of 39°F which shows an external influence from a possible planetary passover.

In 8750 BCE in Ulleungdo we have an eruption. The global field goes down to 7 in 8500 BCE. In 8230 BCE we have the eruption of Grimsvotn, as in 8220 BCE we reach a solar minima. Science has shown a link below sun spots and volcanic activity, as we see a link begin to establish itself. In 8130 BCE we have Taupo erupting again.

A 7560 BCE eruption of the Rotoma Caldera coincides 40 years later in 7520 BCE with a solar minima. The global field increases to ≥8 in 7500 BCE from an external influence. We get a surge in volcanic activity as in 7480 BCE Lvinaya Past erupts, in 7460 BCE Mount Pinatubo erupts, in 7420 BCE Fisher Caldera erupts as well. In 7400 BCE we get the 9.4 Kiloyear event (Erdalen Event) which is a possible impact event that precedes a cooling period. We have solar minimas in 7310 BCE and in 7040 BCE.

In 6940 BCE Mount Vesuvius erupts, while the global magnetic field level is ≥8 in 6556 BCE. In 6440 BCE Kurile Volcano erupts, as in 6400 BCE we reach a solar minima. 6220 BCE sees a solar minima in conjunction in 6200 BCE a Sakurajima eruption, and also in 6200 BCE we have the 8.2 Kiloyear Event that brings a sudden significant cooling period. In 6100 BCE the Storegga Slide causes a megatsunami in the Norwegian Sea. In 6060 BCE Haroharo Caldera erupts, and in 6050 BCE Menengai erupts. We reach the thermal maximum in 6000 BCE as temperatures are the highest in the last 125,000 years with the highest sea levels recorded. We see another sun spot period linked with a major eruption, as in 5990 BCE a solar minima coincides with the major eruption in 5980 BCE of Avachinsky. In 5710 BCE we reach a solar minima in conjunction with an eruption in 5700 BCE of Khangar, and in 5677 BCE a Crater Lake eruption followed in 5620 BCE of a solar minima.

In 5560 BCE we have major eruptions on Mayor Island/Tuhua , in 5550 BCE Tao-Rusyr Caldera erupts, in 5550 BCE Lake Mashu erupts as well. The global magnetic field (difference) falls to ≥7 in 5548 BCE without an eternal influence. In 5500 BCE the Boreal period ends and the Subboreal period begins. In 5260 BCE we have a solar minima.

In 5000 BCE we arrive at the Older Peron Transgression that was a global warm period (unusually warm 5000 BCE to 4000 BCE) that once again is lacking human fingerprints as a cause. In 5000 BCE the Puruogangri Ice Cap: Isotope & Geochemical Date - shows regional temp & moisture variability, as around 5000 BCE the skeleton of the first dark-skinned blue-eyed man is found in Spain.

In 4570 BCE the Merimde culture flourishes along the Nile River, as the global magnetic field increases to ≥8 in 4540 BCE. In 4400 BCE the Amratian/Naqada culture shapes Pre-dynastic Egypt. In 4360 BCE we have an eruption of Macauley Island, in 4350 BCE Kikai Caldera erupts, followed in 4340

BCE by Avachinsky, in 4050 BCE Masaya erupts, and in 4000 BCE Pago finishes up the volcano flurry. We will establish that in 4000 BCE there is a green earth with no deserts, as the model for our proverbial Eden, as the egg has yet to be broken. This period in 4000 BCE has the Egyptian Mystery Religion rise, in 4000 BCE we have the Rise of Sumeria, in 3940 BCE we reach a solar minima, and 3900 BCE brings a 5.9 Kiloyear event. 3750 BCE sees the Pro-Semitic people migrate, and 3630 BCE brings a solar minima.

Another flurry of major volcanic eruptions begins in 3580 BCE as Haroharo Caldera erupts, also in 3580 BCE Taal Volcano erupts, in 3550 BCE Mount Pinatubo erupts, and the global magnetic field level continues to fluctuate at 7 in 3532 BCE. We have the first known Sumerian writing in 3500 BCE, as we reach a solar minima in 3500 BCE as well. 3400 BCE finds the first known Egyptian writing, in 3340 BCE we arrive at a solar minima, and from 3300 BCE to 1300 BCE we have the Indus Valley civilization that was decimated in 2344 BCE.

From 3250 BCE to 3050 BCE we get the Early Dynastic period of Egypt. Egyptian records in 3201 BCE show an event with 70 days of forest fires, rains, flooding, cold temperatures, and with 3,000 Egyptian casualties from a possible meteor strike. In 3200 BCE we have Iron meteor bead jewelry found in the el-Gerzeh cemetery , as the populace began to use the metal falling from the gods, also in 3200 BCE Avachinsky erupts. In 3150 BCE the Scorpion King is Pharaoh, as 3114 BCE sees the start of Maya Time (ended in 2012 & reset), as 12 years later in 3102 BCE we have the start of the Hindu Kali Yuga Age (10,000 yrs end in 6898 CE), 3100 BCE brings the Egyptian Early Dynastic period, and 3100 BCE sees an Upper & Lower Egypt unified kingdom.

The period of 3050 BCE to 2857 BCE is the Egyptian Late Dynastic with an average reign of 19.3 years per Pharaoh. A 3006 BCE event reports 11 days of torrential rain and flooding with 2,600 Egyptian casualties. In 3000 BCE to 2800 BCE Burckle crater is formed in the Indian Ocean from a meteor or comet strike 6 years after a major Egyptian event. We see in 3000 BCE that a 60,000 ton hexagonal rock pile has been found sunken at the bottom of the Sea of Galilee, along the middle of Jordan-Gihon Rift which sits in the middle of the disaster path. In 2860 BCE we reach a solar minima. The Pharaoh's length of reign dips slight by 4.1 years in 2857 BCE to 2705 BCE to 15.2 years average ↓. A reported Egyptian event in 2742 BCE brings us 7 years of famine, cold, dimming Sun, drought, crop failure, famine, and 9,000 Egyptian casualties. I feel that this event has been related as the famines of Ishtar and Inanna, both who represent the planet Venus, and the later Biblical retelling of Joseph and the 7 years of Egyptian famine. In 2705 BCE to 2630 BCE we have the Egyptian Old Kingdom with an average reign of 15 down slightly by 2 months ↓. 2700 BCE brings the rise of the Minoans . We have in 2670 BCE the Battle of Mag Itha, as one of the first recorded wars due to the deteriorating ecosystem. In 2686 BCE the Old Kingdom begins , as around 2600 BCE Stonehenge is built in England, and 2600 BCE sees Sneferu as Pharaoh. The period from 2630 BCE to 2524 BCE sees the reign in Egypt falls 1.75 years to 13.25 years average↓.

The reign in Egypt rises slightly from 2524 BCE to 2400 BCE by .55 years to a 13.7 years average ↑. The wars begin to pick up in 2501 BCE with Mesopotamia/Sumer: Enmebaragesi, Aga, Enmerkar, Dumuzid, Enshakushanna, Eannatum, En-anna-tum, Entemena, and Lugal-Anne-Mundu military campaigns, and in 2500 BCE the Battles of Banquan & Zhuolo are waged. In 2500 BCE the Arroumd *avalanche occurs in High Atlas Mountains from an object with a northwest approach. In 2500 BCE Measles reaches India from Africa, as we begin to see cause in effect with a majority of our modern diseases. Also in 2500 BCE the ancient European dna type haplogroup h is replaced during this period, and also in 2500 BCE to 700 BCE the first Ashkenazi Jewish DNA genetic link is noticed in the Middle East near East-Fertile Crescent.*

In 2494 BCE Egyptian Pyramid religious texts are written during this time. In 2492 BCE we get the Nimrod & Haik war which is the last war 148 years before the egg is broken in 2344 BCE with the Global Flood event. This lack of wars after they had recently started organized warfare, shows that the populace were affected more by the oncoming events than the aggression of their neighbors.

The global magnetic field level rises to ≥8 in 2452 BCE, and in 2420 BCE we Mount Vesuvius erupting. In 2400 BCE a petroglyph in France shows a comet/planet the size of the Atlantic over Greenland, England, & New Foundland which may document a 2492 BCE Passover Event. From 2400 BCE to 2250 BCE we see a rise in Egyptian reign to 18.75 years average ↑.

In 2375 BCE we see Unas as Pharaoh. * 2350 BCE we have the New Madrid Earthquake, which is the very first earthquake on the record for millions of years prior. The impending disaster is influenced by the external force causing earthquakes to begin from parabolic trajectories. In 2350 BCE Unas celebrates the Pharaoh's Jubilee after 25 years of rule, and the first obelisk is built. The word obelisk means Baal's shaft, and symbolizes his penis. This sentiment echoes the Artharva Veda where the Brahmakarin thunders red and white, and spreads his seed across the earth. This concept of the penis of a deity sprinkling semen, also known as manna or mahdu, which was the result of the carbon based content being deposited over the earth ahead of the event. Five years later in 2345 BCE Pharaoh Unas dies, as he is taken before having to see the event unfold, as his son Pepi takes over as Pharaoh. The egg is broken in 2344 BCE as the Great Flood of note unfolds. Egyptian records detail water up to 27.88' deep with 510,000 local casualties. The 2344 BCE event deposited 3000 cubic miles of salt water is to the Black Sea (Black Horse) turning it from a fresh water to a salt water sea. Only an external source would be able to deposit cubic miles of salt to a body of water from above overnight.

The Broken Egg

2300 BCE sees the Sahara begin to form the first desert on earth after the egg is broken and Eden is destroyed. The sudden change in 2300 BCE brings the Neolithic Period to an end in China. **In 2300 BCE the first deserts on earth appear in Egypt?** *In 2300 BCE (or 1300 BCE) we have the Indus Valley civilization collapse. In 2300 BCE the Epic of Gilgamesh and the Enuma Elish are written, as these are some of the earliest retellings of the event. The first war is 49 years after the Great Global Flood Event, as for 194 years total there are no wars. 2295 BCE sees Lugal-zage-si conquers several Sumerian city-states in the first battles after the disaster.*

Egyptian Turmoil Period:

2250 BCE to 2230 BCE: 10 Pharaohs listed (2 yrs. avg.) ↓Unstable
2230 BCE to 2213 BCE: (4.25 yrs. avg.) ↑ Unstable
2213 BCE to 2175 BCE: (19yrs. avg.) Stable ↑

The reign of the Pharaoh is dramatically decreased after the passover event of 2344 BCE that cracked the egg that is the earth. We get an instant drop-off directly after the disaster, as the Pharaoh's of the 6th Dynasty of the Old Kingdom ruled for a healthy average of 18.75 years, but the 7th Dynasty rule bottoms out completely. In 2250 BCE 10 Pharaohs rule in 20 years for a 2 year average. From 2230 BCE to 2213 BCE for a 4.25 average reign per Pharaoh. The period beginning in 2213 BCE sees a return to stability in reign as they average 19 years each.

It has been traditionally presented that the infighting amongst the elite ruling class led to turmoil and murders. These outdated misconceptions must be shelved in order to view things in their true light. A civilization does not achieve the level of mathematics, science, architecture, and theology, that the Egyptians did without cooperation! An individual may prosper through lack of cooperation, but a civilization will never achieve high levels of sophistication without it.

In 2200 BCE not surprisingly the Minoans initiate goddess worship as they understand that it was Venus that demolished the planet. We get yet another strike in 2200 BCE with the 4.2 Kiloyear event, as we also in 2200 BCE get a severe 100 year drought in North Africa, and in 2200 BCE a spike is seen in dolomite samples showing an external deposition.

The 2184 BCE planetary passover has been related as the Sodom and Gomorrah disasters Biblically, as the Dead Sea is summarily destroyed by this event. The sulfur dioxide deposited from Venus scorches the land, leaving a wasteland that our present topography bears witness to. We see in 2181 BCE that the 1st Intermediate Period of Egypt begins after the Sodom and Gomorrah period of destructions in 2814 BCE.

From 2181 BCE to 2169 BCE there are 14 Pharaohs with an average reign of 9 months each during the recorded disasters of Sodom, Gomorrah, Bela/ Zoar,Zeboim, and Admah.

The reign of the Pharaoh increases greatly from 2175 BCE to 2035 BCE for a 28 year per rule. In 2100 BCE the Nile River ceases flowing for 100 to 200 years, as the external force has caused obvious issues with the Moon and the tides. We have the building of the famed Tower of Babel, also known as the Ziggurat of Ur is built in 2100 BCE. I believe that the Ziggurat was built as an observatory on an open plain to track the parabolic trajectory of Venus and the heavenly planets.

2020 BCE brings a rash of major eruptions as Long Island Volcano NE of New Guinea erupts, Changbaishan Volcano in Eastern China erupts, Liamuiga Volcano in the West Indies erupts, and Pago Volcano on New Britain Island erupts as well. There are 4 major eruptions in varied areas of the globe showing it to not be a regional issue. A 2020 BCE event reported by Egyptian records show dimming Sun, cold, drought, crop failure, famine, with around 90,000 Egyptian casualties, as the effects of these eruptions have caused Egypt and other regions to have a nuclear winter, as the sun is blocked on a massive scale .The 2000 BCE GISP2 Greenland Ice Core Ar-N Isotope Temp reconstruction reveals that the snow temperature was actually 30.7C steady, and is 29.9C now which is colder than during that period. This is yet another knock against global warming model! In 2000 BCE the European genetic foundation settles after a major transition. The Biblically related Battle of Siddim takes place in 2000 BCE. From 2000 BCE to 1000 BCE we have the Himalayas continuing the mountain formation process while the Thar region becomes a desert. By 2000 BCE we find that 80% of Egyptian cities are abandoned during this time, as sustaining large populations begin to breakdown the established system. A human skeleton was found in Turkey who's brain was boiled in his skull. This boiling was not found to be caused by fire or through ritual means. Turkey sits at the mouth of the Disaster-Miracle Path, and the damage done can be witnessed by the strange rock formations in Cappadocia. In 2000 BCE we find the first known skeletal evidence of the Biblical scourge leprosy in India. Remember the fall of the Indus Valley and the radioactive levels present there.

From 1991 BCE to 1784 BCE the average reign increases to an amazing 28.875 years ↑. There are 4 Pharaohs during this period with "Amen" in their names, as the Hebrew people enter Egypt around 1917 BCE (Nubkaure Amenemhat II Pharaoh), and one would be thankful to "Amen," for all that he provided. In 1900 BCE the Atrahasis is written, we also see major eruptions in 1900 BCE of Black Peak, in 1890 BCE Mount Hudson erupts, and in 1860 BCE Mount Saint Helens erupts. We have only our second recorded earthquake since the first recorded recent earthquake of 2350 BCE after 519 years in 1831 BCE in Xia China. From 1784 BCE to (1720 BCE?) 1665 BCE the length of reign mysteriously bottoms out once again to 3.44 years average during an unstable period. In 1700 BCE the Rig Vedas are created.

An eggplanation:

Nature has a way of using one thing as a model for other things, as terrestrial planets and eggs seem to fit that mold. The earth and the common egg share similar attributes. The crust of the earth acts as the shell, helping to contain the other layers in orderly fashion, and giving it the round or oval appearance. The upper mantle of the earth can be likened to the outer membrane, and as a supporting layer to the crust/shell. The mantle would provide additional support to the crust and upper mantle, just as the inner membrane of the egg supports the supports the outer membrane and the shell. The outer core of the earth provides the medium for the iron inner core to reside in, just as the egg's inner membrane commonly known as the egg white supports the yolk.

When we hard boil an egg we begin to see the possible answer to the tectonic plate issue. A hot egg cracks more violently than one that has been cooled down. The cracking of the hot egg clearly resembles a similar fracturing process that the earth endured. Once an egg has been broken, we get an extrusion of the inner layers pushing outward. This selfsame process took place when the egg of earth was fractured in 2344 BCE, as the magma that had been sealed began to spew forth through the newly created tectonic plates. The normal processes that occurred within the egg of earth now began to take place on the surface. I feel that volcanic activity is a natural land formation process, but we were not meant to have as many on our surface.

Using the present rate of plate movement of 1.5" per year, and the 2344 BCE start date and up to 2012 would total 4356 years. The 1.5" X 4356 = 6534" ÷ 12" = 544' 5' of plate movement. Based on the dates our movement since the disaster has been minimal. The distance from Brazil in South America to Gabon in Africa is almost 3100 miles. This would indicate an overnight land separation that would have left survivors traumatized for generations to come. The only accurate observation one can make when looking at the seven continents, is that the jigsaw puzzle was broken only recently. In my short lifetime coastlines have changed, with the sand from one beach being deposited to another beach, altering the appearance on the map. The likelihood of the pieces still appearing the same after billions of years is highly improbable.

The oldest rocks found on earth thus far are 3.96 billion years old, yet the solar system is 4.5 billion years old. The tectonic plates destroys the older rocks by pushing them under the plate, rocks are melted and re-melted resetting their internal clocks. Similar fossil records and climate are found in Brazil and Africa, showing this to be a recent connection. We find Australia flooded with poisonous reptiles, while Ireland has few, as land masses separated overnight explosively thus trapping species on particular continents.

Magnetic mapping of the Mid-Atlantic Ridge shows polarity reversals indicating that the floor of the Atlantic Ocean is created at this point due to crustal separation. Magma issues forth and hardens, these new rock are taken either East or West with the older rocks along the North American and European shorelines. This is the method used to date the age of tectonic activity and crustal movement. We again should simply look at the shape of the plate boundary itself between South America and Africa, and we can see that the shape of the plate, is the shape of both continents! Cracked egg? Or cracked theory? You be the judge!

360° to 330° Portion of the Heavens (1/12th)

360° to 330° 17,428 BCE to 15,268 = 2160 years	Age of Scorpio to Age of Libra
Scientific Epoch: Older Dryas stadial	Cold period begins @ 17,000 BCE Pleistocene - started @ 2,588,000 yrs ago
Solfeggio Frequencies: 369/396 to 825/852	Varying range along the scale
Solfeggio Music Note:	F - Sharp and A - Sharp
Volcanic Eruptions:	?
Earthquakes:	?
Geomagnetic Field:	?
Global Population:	?
Dendrochronology:	?
NOAA Ice Core:	?
Disasters:	?
Wars:	?
Rulership:	?
Religion:	?
Texts:	?
Genetics/Sociology: Bands	100,000 to 10,000 years ago - Bands 10's - 100's
Diatonic G 432 Scale factor 9: 360° and 324°	360° - 360° solar point - 360° circle/square sum 3600° = Icosahedron/Dodecahedron sum 324° solar point - 540 hrs mo X 6 mos = 3240 hrs X 2 = 6480 hrs yr X 50 yr Jubilee = 324,000 hrs
Astrology:	360° Alignment and 330° Adjunct
Geometry:	Circle, Square, Icosahedron, and Dodecahedron
Sun Spots:	No Records

*The period from **17,428 BCE (360°)** to **15,268 BCE (330°)** bears scant evidence for texts, religion, rulership, sun spots, and several other categories. This **2160** year period covers the zodiac age of Scorpio transitioning to Libra. This epoch in time shows the beginning of the Older Dryas cold period that began in **17,000 BCE (355°)**, and runs up to **9850 BCE (251°)** point. This cold period runs from the **360°** point to the **299°** degree where the Older Dryas cold period ends. This **2160** year period is completely cold and shows little human activity from available records.*

Human society during this time is composed of bands of people from the tens to the hundreds. These small collectives begin to show the move from sole family groups to the formation of more complex societies.

*The diatonic **432 G** scale has some curious parallels with the celestial degrees and geometry. The **360** degrees of the heavens bears correlation to the sum of a circle or square. The same **360** times **10** equals **3600**, which is equal to the sum of an icosahedrons and a dodecahedrons angles. The important **324°***

*solar point reveals itself when we take an **18** hour day times **30** = **540** hours per month times **6** months = **3240** hours. The **3240** hours times **2** = **6480** hours X **50** year jubilee = **324,000** hours. We begin to see the close relationship that **324** bears to the timekeeping and celestial physics of our universe.*

*The noted astrology points are **360°** which represents attraction, and **330°** which represents an adjunct.*

Geometry: Circle and Square

Circle and Square sum = 360°   "Squaring the Circle"

Geometry and Chemistry: Icosahedron & Dodecaherdon - Platonic Solids - Water & Ether

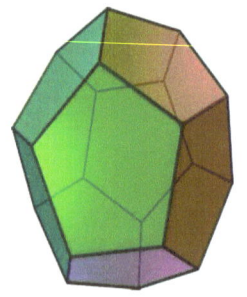 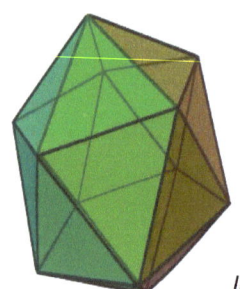

Icosaherdron & Dodecahedron sum = 3600°

Astrology: Age of Scorpio with Mars as planet of rule

Scorpio 360° to 330° Libra   Scorpio symbol - M for Mars with scorpion tail

Mars is the ruling planet for Scorpio and the accompanying male symbol

330° to 300° Portion of the Heavens (2/12th)

330° to 300° 15,268 BCE to 13,108 BCE = 2160 years	Age of Libra to Age of Virgo
Scientific Epoch: Older Dryas stadial	**15,000 BCE to 13,000 BCE** - Cold period
Solfeggio Frequencies: 825/852 to 528	Varying range along the scale
Solfeggio Music Note:	A - Sharp
Volcanic Eruptions:	?
Earthquakes:	?
Geomagnetic Field:	?
Global Population:	?
Dendrochronology:	
NOAA Ice Core:	
Disasters:	?
Wars:	?
Rulership:	?
Religion:	?
Texts:	?
Sociology:	?
Diatonic G 432 Scale factor 9: 306°	**306**,720,000 Solar years = 1 Maha Yuga (Hindu)
Geometry: none	0
Astrology:	**330°** Adjunct, **315°** Quadrate and **300°** Conjunct
Sun Spots:	No Records

The **330°** runs from **15,268 BCE** to the **300°** point in **13,108 BCE**. The cold period of the Older Dryas stadial continues to lower the planets temperature. This **2160** years covers the sign of Libra to the zodiac sign of Virgo.

The diatonic **G 432** scale relates to the **306°** degree of the heavens and the Hindu calendar system. One Maha Yuga on the Hindu calendar is equal **to 306,720,000** solar years. One modern solar year equals @ **394.26** years based on a **24**-hour day, versus the **18**-hour day and **400** solar years of the original celestial design.

Astrology: Age of Libra with Venus as planet of rule

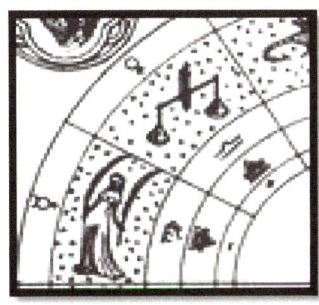

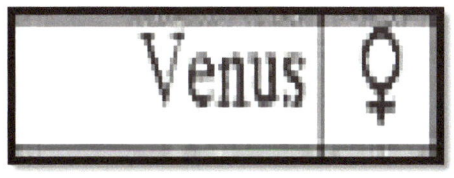

Libra 330° to Virgo 300°   Libra symbol   Libra is ruled by Venus & female symbol

300° to 270° Portion of the Heavens (3/12th)

300° to 270° 13,108 BCE to 10,948 BCE = 2160 years	Age of Virgo to Age of Leo
Scientific Epoch: Older Dryas stadial ends Holocene Epoch begins	13,000 BCE - Cold period ends 13,000 BCE - Warm period begins 12,670 BCE to 1200 BCE - Experienced a warm period & remained stable from 9,200 to 2,500 years ago with a pronounced cooling from 2,500 to 500 years ago - present high rate is unusual known as the Bolling-Allerod Oscillation 12,150 BCE to 11,140 BCE - Mesolithic 2 11,700 BCE - Pleistocene ends 11,700 BCE - Holocene begins 11,700 to 10,800 BCE - Allerod Oscillation 10,900 BCE - Possible Younger Dryas impact event
Solfeggio Frequencies: 528 to 147/174	Varying range along the scale
Solfeggio Music Note:	C - Sharp
Volcanic Eruptions:	?
Earthquakes:	?
Geomagnetic Field:	?
Global Population:	?
Dendrochronology:	0
NOAA Ice Core:	0
Disasters:	11,000 - A northern latitude planetary passover? Meltwater pulse 1A sees sea levels rise **65.7 feet**
Wars:	11,000 - First sign of warfare during Holocene extinction
Rulership:	?
Religion:	?
Texts:	?
Genetics/Sociology:	12,500 BCE to 10,800 BCE - Natufian culture begins minor agriculture 11,000 - massive sudden extinction of megafauna, woolly mammoth, mastodons, and more
Diatonic G 432 Scale factor 9: 288° and 270°	**288°** solar point - **2,88**8,000 days = 1 Piktun (Mayan) **270°** solar point - **540** hrs (month)/ 2 = **270 hrs.** **288 - 270 = 18 the former axis and 18 hour day on earth**
Geometry:	Pentagon
Astrology:	**300°** and **270°**
Sun Spots:	No Records

The **300°** point goes from **13,108 BCE** to **10,948 BCE**. The zodiac sign of Virgo covers the next **2160** years leading to the sign of Leo. This period sees a massive change in global temperature, as the cold period of the Pleistocene ends and the Holocene ushers in a warming trend. A sudden disaster occurs around

11,000 BCE in what has become known as the Holocene extinction. A massive event takes place that kills megafauna, woolly mammoth, mastodons, and more. The first sign of human warfare is seen during the Holocene extinction. The change in climate and resources shows how this massive change pushed humanity to war in the search for needed resources that suddenly were found in short supply. The cool period and resulting warm periods had nothing at all to do with mankind's carbon footprint, as these changes are almost completely the mechanics of how the solar system and Milky Way Galaxy function, in conjunction with periodic internal and external disasters.

The diatonic **G 432** scale shows how the **288°** solar point equates to the **2,888,000** days for **1** Mayan Piktun on the Long Count calendar. The **270°** solar point equates to the totals degrees of a pentagon. The total hours monthly for an **18**-hour day equals **540** divided by **2** equals **270** hours. The same **540** times **12** equals **6480** hours, which equals four zodiac ages in scale of **6480** years. The relationship between **288** and **270** gives us our former axis of the Earth. The pre **2344 BCE** axis was **18°**s and was altered to **23.5°**s after the disastrous planetary passover pushed the Earth down and forward. This change caused the seasons to go from **4/15** (Passover) to **7/4** (Perihelion), the Moon went from **0°**s to **5.5°**s above the planet, and the planet slowed to a **24**-hour day.

The noted astrology points of **300°** and **270°** fall within this portion of the heavens.

Geometry: Pentagon & Tetrahedron (Platonic Solid - Fire)

   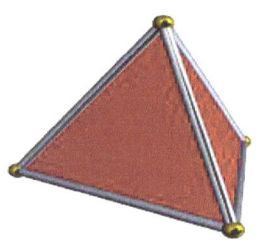

Pentagon sum = 540°   Tetrahedron sum = 540°

Astrology: Age of Virgo with Mercury as the planet of rule (Isis & Horus)

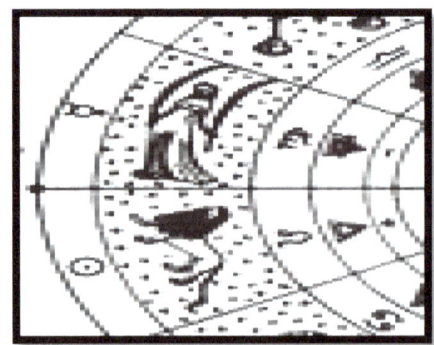      

Virgo 300° to Leo 270°   Astrology symbol for Virgo   Mercury rules the sign of Virgo

270° to 240° Portion of the Heavens (4/12th)

270° to 240° 10,948 BCE to 8788 BCE = 2160 years	Age of Leo to Age of Cancer
Scientific Epoch: **Younger Dryas 10,800 BCE to 9570 BCE** **Preboreal Period 10,300 BCE to 9500BCE**	Warm period begins and ends
Solfeggio Frequencies: 147/174 to 693	Varying range along the scale
Solfeggio Music Note:	C - Sharp
Volcanic Eruptions: Average per 2160 yrs: **720** years	**9650 BCE** - Mt. Tongariro **9460 BCE** - Taupo Volcano (190 YL) **9450 BCE** - Mt. Tongariro (10 YL)
Earthquakes:	?
Geomagnetic Field:	≥8 (10,000 BCE)
Global Population:	?
Dendrochronology:	**9750** - German Oak & Pines
NOAA Ice Core:	**10,800** - West Belukha Plateau - tritium reference horizon, significant sulfate peaks, coincidences with volcanic eruptions, shows Atlai Glacier did not exist during the Bolling-Allerod, suggests air temperature was @ *6.1°s cooler during YD* **10,640** - Grigorieva Ice Cap: coincides with the beginning of the Younger Dryas cold period ice cap did not exist in the Bolling-Allerod warm period - significantly warmer than today **9850** - Wisconsin glaciation advances & retreats - RC dated **9700** - Shows unusually high temperatures in the northern latitudes from **7000** BCE to **4000** BCE **9500 BCE** - Ancylus Lake in the Baltic forms, long-term melting of the Antarctic ice sheet begins **9270 BCE** - Greenland see an abrupt and rapid rise in temperature of *39°F*
Disasters:	**10,000 BCE** - World sea levels rises abruptly with major floods **9500** BCE- Plato's sinking of Atlantis (historical?)
Wars:	?
Rulership:	?
Religion:	?
Texts:	?
Genetics/Sociology: Tribes	10,000 BCE - Neolithic culture begins 9700 BCE - Lake Agassiz reforms from glacial melt-water, Long Island becomes an island, and the Bering Sea cuts off the North American path 8000 BCE to 3000 BCE - Tribes - 100's to 1,000's 9130 to 7370 BCE - Gobekli Tepe, Turkey

Diatonic G 432 Scale factor 9: 270°	270° solar point - 540 hrs / 2 = 270 hrs.
Geometry:	Pentagon (540)
Astrology:	**270°**
Sun Spots:	9170 - Solar minima

The **270°** of **10,948 BCE** to **240°** of **8788 BCE** covers the next **2160** years, and spans the zodiac sign of Leo the lion transitioning to the age of Cancer. This period sees the Younger Dryas cold period begin (**10,800 BCE**) and end (**9570 BCE**), with a brief warm period following suit. The global magnetic field (**GMF**) has been noted to be ≥8 in **10,000 BCE**, and is one of the earliest **GMF** readings found.

The NOAA ice core samples from the West Belukha Plateau (**10,800 BCE**) in Russia shows an increased tritium reference horizon, along with significant sulfate peaks that show a direct relationship with noted volcanic eruptions. The earthquake and volcanic activity bear direct relationships with the celestial physics of our solar system and the Milky Way galaxy. The Atlai Glacier in Russia did not exist during the Bolling-Allerod, which suggests that the air temperature was about **6.1°**s cooler during Younger Dryas cold period. Ice core samples from **10,640 BCE** from the Grigorieva ice cap in Krygyzstan, coincides with the beginning of the Younger Dryas stadial cold period showing that the cap did not exist during the warm period of the Bolling-Allerod warm period, which was significantly warmer than today. In **9850 BCE** the Wisconsin glaciation advances and retreats due to the cold - warm - cold snaps during the era. The ice core samples from **9700 BCE** shows corresponding unusually high temperatures in the northern latitudes from **7000 BCE** to **4000 BCE**. This northern disturbance for those **3000** years suggests a possible periodic parabolic trajectory from a planetary sized object, versus an Earth based event, or that of a solar disturbance.

The only noted disaster of the epoch is that of Plato's much disputed sinking of Atlantis (**9500 BCE**). Much of what Plato having reported has been received as factual, but his sinking of the mythical city will only be accepted if said continent is ever found. This may be the event that caused the massive sinking of the Atlantean continent into the ocean?

The period between **8000 BCE** to **3000 BCE** shows humanity beginning to form larger societies of **100's** of people to **1,000's**. Gobekli Tepe in Turkey has been dated to about **9130 BCE**, and is the oldest known stone city on the planet. The site contains astronomical alignments with many zodiacal creatures. The site was seemingly filled with dirt and abandoned by the inhabitants in **7370 BCE.** I believe that their astronomical observations showed them that they would be in the path of the parabolic trajectory of the planetary passover event to come.

The diatonic **G 432** scale aligns with **the 270°** solar point again aligns with the **540** hours X **12** = **6480** hours or years. The **270°** solar point also equates to the astrology **270°** point, as one is a derivative of the other.

The earliest sun spot record that I was able to find comes from **9170 BCE** and corresponds to a solar minima cold period.

Geometry: Pentagon (Pentagram)

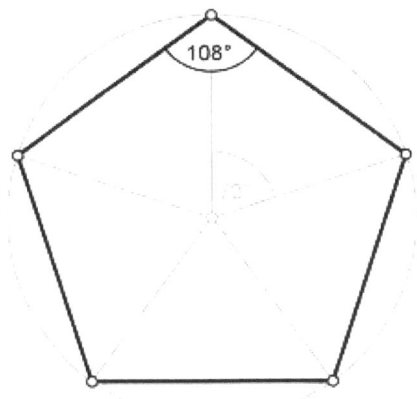

Pentagon sum = 540°

A Pentagram is derived from a Pentagon

Astrology: Age of Leo

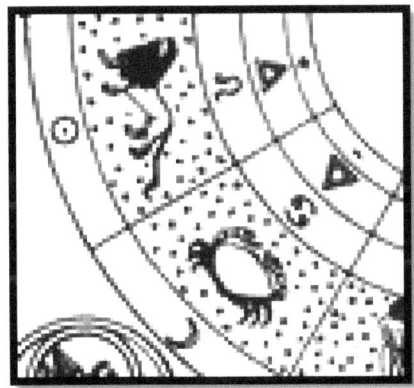

Leo 270° to Cancer 240°

Symbol for Leo

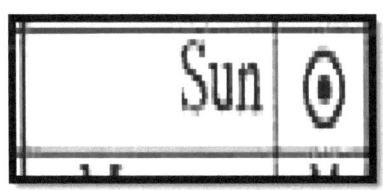

The Sun rules the sing of Leo

240° to 210° Portion of the Heavens (5/12th)

240° to 210° 8788 BCE to 6628 BCE = 2160 years	Age of Cancer to Age of Gemini
Scientific Epoch: Copper Age Boreal Period ends	*6000 BCE* - Chalcolithic (Copper Age) *7000 BCE* - Boreal period begins
Solfeggio Frequencies: 693 to 369/396	Varying range along the scale
Solfeggio Music Note:	C - Sharp High
Volcanic Eruptions:	**8750 BCE** - Ulleungdo **8230 BCE** - Grimsvotn (520 YL) **8130 BCE** - Taupo (100 YL) **7560 BCE** - Rotoma Caldera (570 YL) **7480 BCE** - Lvinaya Past (80 YL) **7460 BCE** - Mt. Pinatubo (20 YL) **7420 BCE** - Fisher Caldera (40 YL) **6940 BCE** - Mt. Vesuvius (480 YL)
Average event per 2160 years: **270 years**	
Earthquakes:	?
Geomagnetic Field:	*7 (8500 BCE)* **and** *≥8 (7500 BCE)*
Global Population:	?
Dendrochronology:	?
NOAA Ice Core:	?
Disasters:	**7400 - 9.4 Kiloyear event (Erdalen Event)** *cooling period*
Wars:	?
Rulership:	?
Religion:	?
Texts:	?
Genetics/Sociology:	?
Diatonic G Scale factor 9: 259° and 216°	*216° solar point* - *216* is half of *432 Frequency scale* *2160°* cube sum *2160* miles Moons diameter *2160* years = 1 Zodiac Age *21,60*0 = 60 mins X 360°/day/year Ezekiel *6:3* (*9*) - *60* cubits X *60* cubits = *3600* cubits or *60* X *60* X *60* = *216,000* 216,000 X 2 = *432*,000 432,000 = 1 Kali Yuga (Hindu) *25,92*0 yrs. = 1 Zodiac Age (12 X *2160*) / *6480* yrs X 4 = *25,920* yrs *2,592*,000 miles Earth to Moon - *2,592*,000 hrs / *360* = *72*00 hrs / *18* hrs = *400* Tropical Yrs *259,2*00,000 yrs = 1 Brahma month
Geometry:	Cube (*2160*)
Astrology:	N/A

Sun Spots:	*8220 - Solar minima*
	7520 - Solar minima (700yrs later)
	7310 - Solar minima (210yrs later)
	7040 - Solar minima (270yrs later)
	Average: 540 years per

*The **240°** of **8788 BCE** to **210°** of **6628 BCE** covers the **2160** years of the zodiac age of Gemini up to the age of Taurus. The Boreal warm period begins around **7000 BCE**. **6000 BCE** begins the Chalcolithic Age also known as the Copper Age. The global magnetic field rises from **7** to **≥8** during this **2160** year period.*

*The diatonic **G 432** scale shows us how important this portion of the heavens is to celestial physics and geometry. The **216°** solar point relates to exactly half of the original Pythagorean **432** Diatonic G musical scale, and this relationship bears itself out on many levels. The **216°** times **10** = **2160°**s, which is equal to the sum of a cube's angles. This relationship to the Cube plays itself out in our the religions of Judaism and Islam. The male Jewish faithful wear a small black cube known as a tefillin on their foreheads, while the Islamic faithful circumambulate a black cube known as the Kabaa in emulation of the zodiac traveling the left-hand path of the heavens. The diameter of the Moon is **2160** miles showing the veneration the ancients established for the lesser light in the sky, as the Hebrew and Babylonian calendars are luni-solar. One zodiac age equals **2160** years (Pisces, Aquarius, etc.). Twelve zodiac ages (**12 X 2160**) times **2160** equals **25,920**, or **1** complete Zodiac Cycle. The same **25,920** divided by **4** equals **6480** years. When we take our same **25,920** years and convert it to miles times **100** = **2,592,000** miles, which is equal to the distance of the Earth to the Moon. The Earth also travels **2,592,000** miles each day on our journey through the solar system. When we take that **2,592,000** as hours, and divide it by **360** we get **7200** hours, and then divide it by an **18** hour day we get **400** Tropical Years. Our **259,200,000** years is equal to one Hindu Brahma month. The Great Pyramid of Giza was originally lined with 144,000 exterior casing stones with **8** concave sides, that recorded the passage of time in **400** year increments with that particular use of the pyramid. Ezekiel **6:3** states that the new temple should be **60 X 60** cubits, but leaves out the **3rd** dimension, which would also be cubits. This dimension gives us **60 X 60 X 60** = **216,000** cubits, which is half of a Kali Yuga **432,000** year age, **216°** solar point, **2160°** sum of a square, **2160** miles of the Moon's diameter, and **2160** years equal **1** zodiac age. The only other geometric object close to those dimensions is the equilateral triangle of **60°** + **60°** + **60°** = **180** sum.*

*This period shows an excellent record for sun spots, as we reach solar minima in **8220 BCE, 7520 BCE, 7310 BCE,** and in **7040 BCE**. These sun spots minimums show a correlation with reduced global temperatures.*

Geometry: Cube - Platonic Solid (Earth)

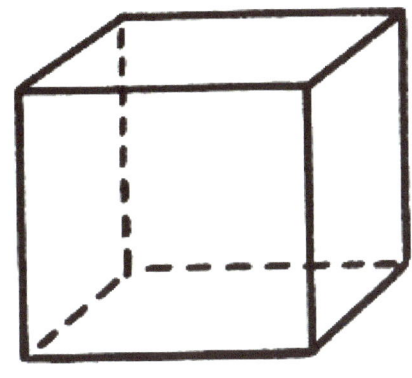

Cube sum = 2160°

2160 miles = Moons diameter

216° solar point

2160 miles = Moons diameter

2160 years = 1 Zodiac Age

2160 X 12 = 25,920 = 1 Complete Zodiac Cycle

25,920 X 100 = 2,292,000 miles equal to the distance the Earth travels daily

Astrology: Age of Cancer

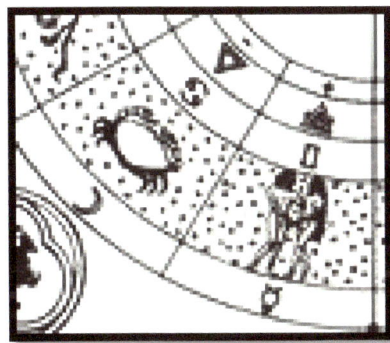

Cancer 240° to Gemini 210°

Cancer symbol (tidal lock?)

The Moon rules Cancer and the Cube

210° to 180° Portion of the Heavens (6/12th)

210° to 180° 6628 BCE to 4468 BCE = 2160 years	Age of Gemini to Age of Taurus
Scientific Epoch: Boreal Period Subboreal	**6000 BCE** - **Thermal maximum** is reached as temperatures are the **highest** in the last **125,000** years and with the highest sea levels **5000 BCE** - Older Peron Transgression - global warm period (unusually warm **5000 BCE to 4000 BCE**) **5500 BCE** - Boreal period ends **5500 BCE** - Subboreal period begins
Solfeggio Frequencies: 369/396 to 825/852	Varying range along the scale
Solfeggio Music Note:	F - Sharp
Volcanic Eruptions:	**6440 BCE** - Kurile Volcano **6200 BCE** - Sakurajima (240 YL) **6060 BCE** - Haroharo Caldera (140 YL) **6050 BCE** - Menengai (10 YL) **5980 BCE** - Avachinsky (70 YL) **5700 BCE** - Khangar (280 YL) **5677 BCE** - Crater Lake (23 YL) **5560 BCE** - Mayor Island/Tuhua (117 YL) **5550 BCE** - Tao-Rusyr Caldera (10 YL) **5550 BCE** - Lake Mashu **5250 BCE** - Mt. Aniakchak (330 YL) **4750 BCE** - Mt. Hudson (500 YL)
Average event per 2160 years: **180 years**	
Earthquakes:	?
Geomagnetic Field:	≥8 (6556 BCE), ≥7 (5548 BCE), and ≥8 (4540 BCE)
Global Population:	**5** to **20** million
Dendrochronology:	5690 - Neolithic Lake Bracciano Settlement (oak pilings in anoxic lake-bottom sediments)
NOAA Ice Core:	5000 - Puruogangri Ice Cap: Isotope & Geochemical Date - regional temp & moisture variability
Disasters:	**6200 BCE** - **8.2 Kiloyear Event** - a sudden significant cooling **6100 BCE** - Storegga Slide causes a megatsunami in the Norwegian Sea
Wars:	?
Rulership:	?
Religion:	**5500 BCE** - Proto Indo-Europeans - sacrificial idology religion **5200 BCE** - Time of Hindu Lord Rama
Texts:	?
Genetics/Sociology:	@ **5000 BCE** the first dark-skinned blue-eyed man found in Spain
Astrology Point: 210° and 180°	Semi-Sextile and Opposition

Diatonic G 432 Scale factor 9: 180°	180° solar point - 180° equilateral triangle sum
Geometry:	Triangle
Sun Spots:	6400 - Solar minima
	6220 - Solar minima (180yrs later)
	5990 - Solar minima (230yrs later)
	5710 - Solar minima (280yrs later)
	5620 - Solar minima (90yrs later)
	5260 - Solar minima (360yrs later)
	(190 year avg.)

*The midway point of **210° (6628 BCE)** to **180° (4468 BCE)** finds us in the Age of Gemini, and an end to the warm Boreal period in **5500 BCE**, and the beginning of the Subboreal cold period. The global magnetic field rides a wave during this pre-disaster period. The field is ≥8 in 6556 BCE, then lowers to ≥7 (5548 BCE), and then rises back to ≥8 (4540 BCE), and brings in to question what force is causing the rising and dropping of the GMF.*

*The global population is between **5** and **20** million people around **5000 BCE**, as the first dark-skinned blue-eyed man was recently unearthed in Spain from that time. This shows people from Africa in these regions much earlier than noted, and with the curious anomaly of having blue eyes. It has been noted that the earliest green eyed ancestor appeared around **6000 BCE**, and that all blue-eyed and green-eyed people share a common ancestor. This finding in Spain may begin to change our views on genetics and heredity?*

*The samples of dendrochronolgy take from Lake Bracciano in Italy, taken shows a settlement from oak pilings in the anoxic (oxygen starved) lake, which would not have been conducive to humans having a settlement based around it. Lakes and bodies of water may become anoxic from farming, and this also naturally occurs, but the people were just beginning to cultivate the land, so this would not have resulted from over-farming the land. Three main anoxic lake are exist on the planet, and all three reside in the **Disaster-Miracle Path (DMP)**; Baltic Sea, Gulf of Mexico, and Hood Canal (Washington state).*

*The NOAA ice core samples from the Puruogangri Ice Cap in the Tibetan Plateau, through isotope and geochemical data a variability in regional temperature and moisture in **5000 BCE**.*

*The Kurile Volcano in Russia erupts in **6440 BCE**, which precedes the solar minima of **6400 BCE** indicating a direct relationship between global and solar events.*

*The planet reaches the Thermal Maximum in **6000 BCE**, bringing the warmest temperatures in **125,000** years. Mankind bore no footprint of fossil fuel use at this point of civilization, yet some internal force, external force, or a combination of both, raises the global temperature to unprecedented levels. While we must reduce our footprint on the planet in many ways, these past epochs show us that these events will occur without our assistance. The **8.2 Kiloyear Event** causes a sudden and rapid dip in global temperature. The theory is that the Laurentide ice shelf finally collapsed, sending meltwater into the Northern Atlantic raising global water levels.*

*The sun spots solar minima cold periods occurred on; **6400 BCE, 6220 BCE, 5990 BCE, 5710 BCE, 5620 BCE**, and **5260 BCE**, with an average of **190** years between events.*

*Religion as a formal discipline is first shown in **5500 BCE**, as the Proto Indo-Europeans begin a theology based around sacrifices and idology. The time of Hindu Lord Rama occurs in **5200 BCE**.*

*The diatonic **G 432** scale shows relationship to the **180°** solar point, as well as the geometry related to the sum of an equilateral triangle **(180°)**. The astrology points noted are the **210°** is semi-sextile, and the **180°** is Opposition.*

Geometry: Equilateral Triangle

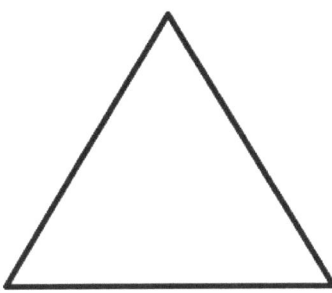

Triangle sum = 180° (venerated & revered worldwide)

Astrology: Age of Gemini

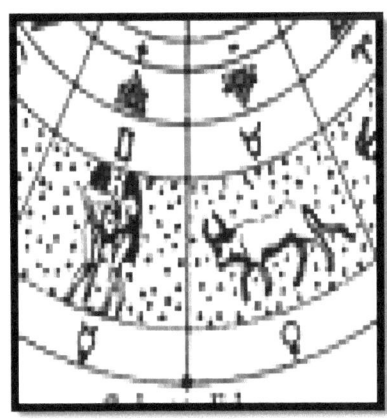 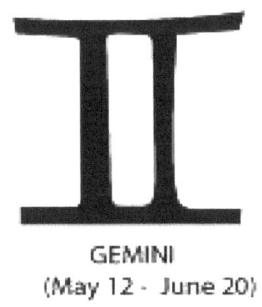 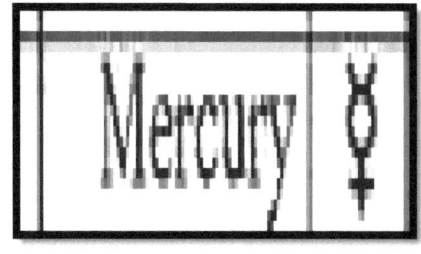

Gemini 210° to Taurus 180°   *Gemini twin symbol*   *Mercury rules the sign of Gemini*

180° to 150° Portion of the Heavens (7/12th)

180° to 150° 4468 BCE to 2308 BCE = 2160 years	Age of Taurus to Age of Aries
Scientific Epoch: Holocene	Ongoing **3500 BCE to 3000 BCE** - Neolithic subpluvial
Solfeggio Frequencies: 825/852 to 528	Varying range along the scale
Solfeggio Music Note:	F - Sharp
Volcanic Eruptions: Average per 2160 years: **216 years**	**4360 BCE** - Macauley Island **4350 BCE** - Kikai Caldera (10 YL) **4340 BCE** - Avachinsky (10 YL) **4050 BCE** - Masaya (290 YL) **4000 BCE** - Pago (50 YL) **3580 BCE** - Haroharo Caldera (420 YL) **3580 BCE** - Taal Volcano **3550 BCE** - Mt. Pinatubo (30 YL) **3200 BCE** - Avachinsky (350 YL) **2420 BCE** - Mt. Vesuvius (780 YL)
Earthquakes: *1 noted EQ in 2160 years*	**2350 - New Madrid Earthquake**
Geomagnetic Field:	**7 (3532 BCE) and ≥8 (2452 BCE)**
Global Population:	20 million +
Dendrochronology:	**3607** - The Sweet Track ancient timber roadway in England **3374** - Arsslantepe-Malatya cylinder seal with threshing board or sledge image (tree ring dating)
NOAA Ice Core:	**4000** - GISP2 Ice Core Ar-N-Isotope Temp. Reconstruction
Disasters:	**4000** - Green Earth with no deserts**?** **3900 BCE** - 5.9 Kiloyear event **3201** event- **70** days of forest fires, rains, flooding, cold temperatures, and **3,000** Egyptian casualties **3200** - Iron meteor bead jewelry found in el-Gerzeh cemetery **3006** event - **11** days of torrential rain & flooding with **2,600** Egyptian casualties (195 YL) **@ 3000 to 2800** - Burckle crater is formed in the Indian Ocean from a meteor or comet strike (6 YL) **3000** - A **60,000** ton hexagonal rock pile sunken at the bottom of the Sea of Galilee **2742 event - 7 years of famine**, cold, dimming Sun, drought, crop failure, famine, and **9,000** Egyptian casualties (Ishtar, Inanna, & Joseph's 7yrs of famine tale) (258 YL) **2500** - Arroumd avalanche; High Atlas Mountains NW **2500** - Measles reaches India from Africa **2400** - Petroglyph in France shows a comet/planet the size

	of the Atlantic over Greenland, England, & New Foundland (**2492 BCE Passover Event?**) **2344** - Pepi Pharaoh of the Great Flood (**27.88' deep - 510,000** local casualties) (398 YL) **3,000 cubic miles** of salt water is added to the Black Sea (Black Horse) turning it from a fresh water to a salt water sea. The Sahara and other deserts begin to form during this period **@ 1200 to 800** - Greek Dark Ages
Wars: Average per 2160 years: **166.15 years**	**2670** - Battle of Mag Itha **2501** - Mesopotamia/Sumer: Enmebaragesi, Aga, Enmerkar, Dumuzid, Enshakushanna, Eannatum, En-anna-tum, Entemena, and Lugal-Anne-Mundu (169 yrs later) **2500** - Battles of Banquan & Zhuolo (1 yr later) **2492** - Nimrod & Haik war (8 yrs later) **2344 Event** - (No wars noted 148 years before & 49 years after = 197 years)
Rulership:	**4000** - Rise of Sumeria **3150** - Scorpion King Pharaoh **3100** - Egyptian Early Dynastic **3100** - Upper & Lower Egypt unified kingdom **2740** - Pyramids aligned /Khasekhmwy Pharaoh **2700** - Minoans rise **2686** - Old Kingdom begins **@ 2600** - Stonehenge built **2600** - Sneferu Pharaoh **2490 - 2477 BCE** - Sahure Pharaoh 5th Dynasty **2450** - Neferefre Pharaoh **2375** - Unas Pharaoh **2350** - Unas Pharaoh's Jubilee obelisk built **2345** - Pharaoh Unas dies **2345** - Pepi becomes Pharaoh **2344** - Great Flood of note
Religion:	**4000** - Egyptian Mystery Religion **3750** - Pro-Semitic people migrate **2200** - Minoans initiate goddess worship **1700** - Rig Vedas created **@ 1367** - Ahkenaten begins a monotheistic Sun religion
Texts:	**3114** - Start f Maya Time (ends in 2012 & resets) **3102** - Start of Hindu Kali Yuga (10,000 yrs end in 6898 CE) **2494** - Egyptian Pyramid religious texts
Genetics/Sociology: Chiefdoms	**3000 to 1000 BCE** - Chiefdom's - 1,000's to 10,000's **4570** - Merimde culture Nile River **4400** - Amratian/Naqada culture Pre-dynastic Egypt **3500** - 1st Sumerian writing **3400** - 1st Egyptian Writing

	3300 to 1300 - Indus Valley civilization **2500** - Ancient European dna type haplogroup h is replaced during this period **2500 BCE to 700 BCE**- *First Ashkenazi Jew DNA genetic link in the Middle East (Near East-Fertile Crescent aka BABYLON!!!)*
Astrology Point: 180° and 150°	Opposition and inconjunct
Diatonic G 432 Scale factor 9: 180° and 162°	180° solar point - 180° triangle sum 1620 hrs = 540 X 3 (540° = pentagon sum)
Geometry:	Equilateral Triangle
Sun Spots:	3940 - Solar minima 3630 - Solar minima (310 years later) 3500 - Solar minima (130 years later) 3340 - Solar minima (160 years later) 2860 - Solar minima (480 years later) **216 year average**
Average length of Pharaoh's rule: 10 Pharaohs named Horus 7 Pharaohs named Horus 5 Pharaohs named Horus	3250 - 3050: Early Dynastic 3050 - 2857: Late Dynastic (19.3 yrs. avg.) 2857 - 2705: (15.2 yrs. avg.) ↓ 2705 - 2630: Old Kingdom (15 yrs. avg.) ↓ 2630 - 2524: (13.25 yrs. avg.) ↓ 2524 - 2400: (13.7 yrs. avg.) ↑ 2400 - 2250: (18.75 yrs. avg.) ↑ **Unas Pharaoh 2375 - 2345 Teti Pharaoh 2345 - 2333** **Global Flood 2344**
Mayan World Sun: 1st World Sun: Jaguar Sun (Sun Spots!) 2344	Tezcatlipoca: Becomes half a Sun creates giants and gives them acorns (meteorites) to eat - Great Flood era Gen. 6:4, Enoch 7:3, Numbers 13:33, Deut. 2:11

*The period of **180° (4468 BCE)** to **150° (2308 BCE)** covers the Age of Taurus preceding the Age of Aries, and this is very important in understanding the disasters, onset of theologies, wars, leadership upheaval, and other factors that contribute to our present paradigm. I will break this into four portions of **540** years each to see how the parabolic pass-overs begin to affect humanity, as the trajectory brings it closer to an exchange between two similarly sized and oppositely charged planets (Earth **(-)** and Venus **(+)**).*

4468 BCE to 3928 BCE (180° to 172.5°)

4570 BCE *sees the Merimde culture rise on the banks of the Nile River.* ***4400 BCE*** *brings the rise of the Amratian/Naqada culture of Pre-dynastic Egypt.* ***4000 BCE*** *has us with a green Earth and no deserts, as we now know that the first desert on the planet was the Sahara desert that began to form around* ***2300 BCE****, and not over the course of millions of years as previously taught. This same inaccurate desertification model can still be found in our textbooks and being taught in our classrooms. If the*

Sahara was the first desert, then we must ask what level disaster brought this about? **4000 BCE** *sees the rise of the Egyptian Mystery Religion and the rise of the Sumerian Kingdom. The* **3940 BCE** *solar minima cold period see the* **GMF** *level at* **7** *in* **3532 BCE** *with a global population around* **20 million**.

3928 BCE to 3388 BCE (172.5° to 165°)

3750 BCE *sees the eventual Proto-Semitic people migrate to the Middle East region. We have in* **3500 BCE** *the first known Sumerian writing, with the first known Egyptian writing in* **3400 BCE**. *In* **3630 BCE** *and in* **3500 BCE** *we reach cold periods of solar minima.*

3388 BCE to 2848 BCE (165° to 157.5°)

In **3500 BCE** *we have a solar minima, and another in solar minima in* **3340 BCE**. *In* **3250 BCE - 3050 BCE** *we have the rise of the Early Dynastic period in Egypt.* **3300 BCE** *has the rise of the Indus Valley civilization that eventually falls in* **1300 BCE** (**1730** *yrs*) *during the post - Exodus disasters.* **3200** *- Iron meteor bead jewelry found in el-Gerzeh cemetery.* **3150 BCE** *has the Scorpion King as Pharaoh. Mayan time starts in* **3114 BCE** *and consists of* **13 Baktuns** *of* **144,000** *days each, this calendar found completion in* **2012 CE**, *and then reset to start anew. The Hindu calendar began a special* **10,000** *year Kali Yuga in* **3102 BCE**, *and this calendar ends in* **6898 BCE**, *when Ophiuchus (Serpent Bearer, Balarama, Lord Krishna) steps on the stinger of the Scorpio constellation. Egyptian records show a* **3201 BCE** *event of* **70** *days of forest fires, rains, flooding, cold temperatures, and* **3,000** *Egyptian casualties.* **3100 BCE** *has the rise of the Egyptian Early Dynastic period along with Upper & Lower Egypt becoming a unified kingdom. The period of* **3050 BCE- 2857 BCE** *covers the Late Dynastic period in Egypt, and shows a very stable length of rule of* **19.3** *years average. Egyptian records show a* **3006 BCE** *event with* **11** *days of torrential rain and flooding with* **2,600** *Egyptian casualties*

The period from **3000 BCE** *to* **1000 BCE** *sees humanity grouping in social structures of Chiefdom's in the* **1,000's** *to the* **10,000's**. *Around* **3000 BCE to 2800 BCE** *Burckle crater is formed in the Indian Ocean from a meteor or comet strike, as we see these events begin to pick up frequency. A* **60,000** *ton hexagonal shaped rock pile from* **3000 BCE** *sits at the bottom of the Sea of Galilee directly on the Jordan-Gihon fault line.*

2848 BCE to 2416 BCE (157.5° to 151°)

We enter the disaster period in **2860 BCE** *with a solar minima cold period. The length of rule of the Pharaoh dips slightly in the* **2857 BCE - 2705 BCE: (15.2 yrs. avg.)** ↓ *era by* **4.3** *years. The Egyptian reported* **2742 BCE** *event of* **7 years of famine, cold, dimming Sun, drought, crop failure, famine**, *and* **9,000 Egyptian casualties,** *these events show the effects from the onset of* **parabolic (parables) trajectories**. *The events related from these documents become the basis for the Egyptian tale of Ishtar (***Venus***) and the Bull of Heaven (Taurus), the Sumerian story of Innana (***Venus***) and the 7 Year Famine, the Biblical tale of Zaphenath Paneah aka Joseph, as he was an Egyptian high priest the bulk of his life, and the story would be a later retelling of the older tales from much fabled lands that they resided in at times.* **2740 BCE** *is my personal dating for the alignment of the pyramids during Khasekhmwy reign, as it is almost exactly* **1** *Solar year (***396** *years) from the big event* **of 2344 BCE**. *The length of reign from* **2705**

BCE - 2630 BCE *sees the Old Kingdom hold consistent with only a **.02** dip (**15** yrs. avg.) ↓ versus the prior kingdom. The Minoan kingdom rises in the Mediterranean in **2700 BCE**. The Egyptian Old Kingdom begins in **2686 BCE**. In **2670 BCE** the Battle of Mag Itha is waged. The Egyptian Old Kingdom runs from **2630 BCE - 2524 BCE**: (**13.25** yrs. avg.) ↓ and shows another very slight decline of 1.75 years. Stonehenge is built around **2600 BCE** in present day England. In **2600 BCE** we have- Sneferu as pharaoh. The Egyptian kingdom period of **2524 BCE - 2400 BCE** sees a very slight increase in the length of reign of **.18** months (**13.7** yrs. avg.)↑. The Arrroumd avalanche occurs in **2500 BCE**, as the northwest face has a rock pile that a village rests upon. It was theorized that the rock pile was the result of glacial melt, but that premise was proven inaccurate. The new premise is that glacial erosion "probably" caused the pile, as the researchers were surprised to find out how young the pile actually was. As I have shown in other works and with this project, Morocco sits in the parabolic trajectory path also known as the Biblical Disaster-Miracle Path (DMP). The bulk of the earth's deserts and strange natural (unnatural) formations rest. The rock pile rests on the northwest side of the mountain, which gives an indicator that the force came from the northwest. The Great Pyramid of Giza is slightly tilted to the northwest, and this northeast approach of Venus is commemorated in the practice of setting the cornerstone to the northwest in Masonic and architectural designs. **2501 BCE** finds Mesopotamia/Sumer enmeshed in a series of wars and campaigns as upheaval begins to set in with the following wars: Enmebaragesi, Aga, Enmerkar, Dumuzid, Enshakushanna, Eannatum, En-anna-tum, Entemena, and Lugal-Anne-Mundu. The Battles of Banquan and Zhuolo are fought in China in **2500 BCE**. In **2500 BCE** measles reaches the Indian continent during this period of biological turmoil. The ancient European dna type haplogroup h is replaced during this period possibly due to the onset of climatic conditions prior to the event some **3** Jubilee passovers (**50** yrs. each) later. **2500 BCE to 700 BCE** sees the first Ashkenazi Jew DNA genetic link in the Middle East (Near East-Fertile Crescent aka BABYLON). The Egyptian Pyramid religious texts date back to **2494 BCE**. In **2492 BCE** the Nimrod & Haik war occurs. This is the last war prior to the passover event **148** years later in **2344 BCE**. The global magnetic field sits at ≥8 in**2452 BCE**. In **2490 BCE- 2477 BCE** we have Sahure as Pharaoh of the **5th** Dynasty, in **2450 BCE** we have Neferefre as Pharaoh.*

2416 BCE to 2345 BCE - Onset of Global Flood Event

*A petroglyph (DeJonge) in France shows a comet/planet with a swath the size of the Atlantic Ocean passing over; Greenland, Great Britain, and New Foundland, around **2400 BCE (2492 BCE Passover Event?)**. Peoples around the globe give well documented examples of what was occurring to their planet. The length of reign during this period increases **2400 BCE - 2250 BCE** (**18.75** yrs. avg.) ↑ an increase of **5.05** years. The reign of Unas as Pharaoh begins in **2375 BCE**. For the Pharaoh's Jubilee during the reign of Unas an obelisk is built to commemorate the **50** year passage of time in **2350 BCE**. The use of the obelisk represents the ejection disk that was emitted by the comet **Venus**, as obelisk is translated as Baal's shaft (penis). The New Madrid fault line contributes to a massive earthquake in **2350 BCE**, as the parabolic trajectory of Venus tugs at the Earth causing a major eruption. The Pharaoh Unas dies in **2345 BCE** due to the onset of the event to come as his son Teti takes over as Pharaoh one year prior to the event.*

2344 -150.5° Great Flood of note

*Teti is pharaoh during the global disaster event of **2344 BCE** (**27.88'** deep - **510,000** local casualties), as **3000 cubic miles** of salt water is added to the **Black Sea (Black Horse)** turning it from a fresh water sea to a salt water sea. The Sahara and other deserts begin to form during this period. Teti passes in **2334 BCE** as this period begins the birth of major issues globally.*

2343 BCE - 2308 BCE 150.5° to 150° Inconjunct

Geometry: Equilateral Triangle

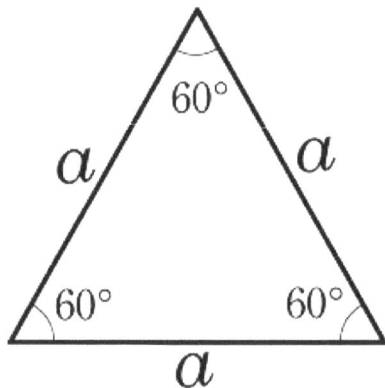

Equilateral triangle sum = 180°

Astrology: Age of Taurus

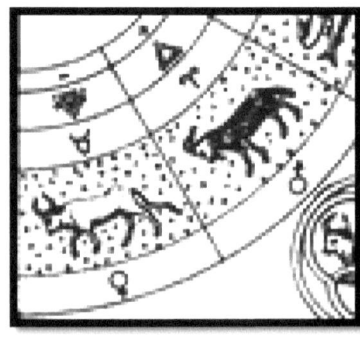

Taurus 180° to Aries 150°

Taurus symbol

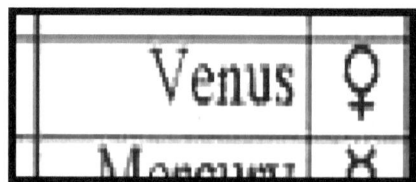

Venus rules the sign of Taurus

150° to 120° Portion of the Heavens (8/12th)

150° to 120° 2308 BCE to 148 BCE = 2160 years	Age of Aries to Age of Pisces
Scientific Epoch: Subboreal Subatlantic	2300 BCE - Neolithic Period ends in China 500 BCE - Subboreal period ends 500 BCE - Subatlantic period begins
Solfeggio Frequencies: 528 to 147/174	Varying range along the scale
Solfeggio Music Note:	F - Sharp High
Volcanic Eruptions: Volcano average 2160 years: **120 years**	*2020 BCE Long Island Volcano: NE of New Guinea, Changbaishan Volcano: Eastern China Liamuiga Volcano: West Indies Pago Volcano- New Britain Island* **1900 BCE** - Black Peak (120 YL) **1890 BCE** - Mt. Hudson (10 YL) **1860 BCE** - Mt. Saint Helens (30 YL) **1750 BCE** - Mt. Veniaminof (110 YL) **1645 BCE** - Mt. Aniakchak (105 YL) **1610 BCE** - Youngest Caldera, Santorini (35 YL) **1500 BCE** - Avachinsky (110 YL) **1460 BCE** - Taupo Volcano (40 YL) **1370 BCE** - Pago Volcano (90 YL) **1350 BCE** - Avachinsky (20 YL) **1050 BCE** - Mt. Pinatubo (300 YL) **550 BCE** - Mt. Tongariro (500 YL) **400 BCE** - Mt. Meager (150 YL) **250 BCE** - Raoul Island (150 YL
Earthquakes: Earthquake average: 720 years	**1831 BCE** - Xia China EQ **464 BCE** - Sparta Greece EQ (1367 YL) **226 BCE** - Rhodes Greece EQ (238 YL)
Geomagnetic Field:	*9 (1588 BCE), and ≤11 (1012 BCE)*
Global Population:	27 million to 100 million
Dendrochronology:	**2300** - **A1 and A2 date periods for Unetice culture Europe** **2049** - Seahenge constructed in Britain **1300** - Oxide ingot from Uluburun shipwreck from south coast of Turkey **148** - Corlea Trackway Ireland
NOA Ice Core:	**2000** - GISP2 Greenland Ice Core Ar-N Isotope Temp reconstruction: snow temp was *30.7C* steady & is *29.9C* now which is colder *(NO Global Warming!)* **500** - WAIS Divide Ice Core 1500 Year Sulfate & Nitrogen Isotope Data **520** - Dunde Ice Core 1500 Year d180, Dust, Anion, and Accumulation Data - abrupt change corresponds to structural changes in civilizations
Disasters:	**2300** - First deserts on earth appear in Egypt? **2300** - Indus Valley Collapses **2200** - 4.2 Kiloyear event

	2200 - Severe *100* year drought North Africa *2200* - Spike seen in dolomite samples *2184* - Planetary passover related as the Sodom & Gomorrah disasters *2181* - 1st Intermediate begins after the Sodom & Gomorrah period of destructions in *2814 BCE* *2100* - Nile River ceases flowing for *100 to 200* years *2020* event - dimming Sun, cold, drought, crop failure, famine, with @ *90,000* Egyptian casualties *2000 to 1000* - Himalayas continued formation, Thar region becomes desert *2000* - *80%* of Egyptian cities are abandoned at this time *2000* - Human found in Turkey who's brain had been boiled in his skull *2000* - First skeletal evidence of leprosy in India *1628* event - *9 to 10* days of forest fires & floods - global event *1500* - Dwarka sinks into the sea *1500* - Santorini sinks into the sea *1450* - Mediterranean 300 year drought starts *1370* event - *50* days of dimming Sun, *2* years of dust in the skies, *7* years of famine: *3* phases, dimming Sun, cold, drought, crop failure, famine, *950,000* global casualties *1200 BCE to 800 BCE* - Greek Dark Ages *1159* event - *40* and *40* days *80* total, torrential rain, cold, floods, forest fires, *5.8* million global casualties: Dardanus Flood (after *1194* event), *3.8* million global casualties, *18'* of water *1150* - Meditteranean drought ends *1000* - First sign of smallpox in Egypt *800* - **2.8 Kiloyear Event** *430* event - *13* days of forest fires, flooding, rain, and *830,000* local casualties *207* event - *8* days of forests fires, floods, and rain, with *530,000* local casualties
Wars:	*First war 49 years after the Great Global Flood Event 194 years total no wars* *2295* - Lugal-zage-si conquers several Sumerian city-states *2150* - Glutian attacks on Akkad (145 YL) *2047 to 2030* - Ur-Nammu (Lagash) (103 yrs later) *2000* - Battle of Siddim (30 yrs. later) *1940* - Elamites sack Ur (60 yrs later) *1830 to 1817* - Amorite independence (90 yrs later) *1752 to 1730* - Damiq-ilishu defeated by Sin-Muballit of Babylon (65 yrs later) *1728* - Hammurabi of Babylon rules (2 yrs later) *1650 to 1600* -Hattusili & Mursili defeated (78 yrs later) *1628 to 1600* - Shang conflict (22 yrs later)

1600 - *Hyksos invade Lower Egypt*
1600 - *Battle of Mingtiao*
1507 - Kassites attack Babylon (93 yrs later)
1487 Event no wars 20 years before event - no wars 30 years after event (1 Jubilee planetary passover of 49 years) Exodus disasters end 1447
1457 - Tuthmosis III wins the Battle of Megiddo with Canaanite help (50 yrs later) *First war after Exodus event*
1430 - Kaska invasion of Hatti starts (27 yrs later)
1400 - Battle of Ai (30 yrs later)
1400 - Battle of the 10 Kings
1350 - Kaska invasions of Hatti end (50 yrs later)
1279-1213 - Ramesses II Near East campaign (71 yrs later)
1274 - Egyptian Battle of Kadesh (5 yrs later)
1260 to 1240 - Trojan war (14 yrs later)
1232-1225 - Tukulti-Ninurta 1 Assyrian supremacy over Babylon (28 yrs later)
1200 - Kurukshetra war starts (25 yrs later)
1046 - Battle of Muye (154 yrs later)
1000 - Seige of Jebus (46 yrs later)
740 - Start 1st Messenian war (260 yrs later)
720 - End 1st Messenian war (20 yrs later)
710 - Lelantine war starts (10 yrs later)
701 - Sennacherib's campaigns (9 yrs later)
685 - 2nd Messenian war begins (16 yrs later)
668 - 2nd Messenian war ends (17 yrs later)
650 - Lelantine war ends (18 yrs later)
* Biblical Babylonian Exile period 580 BCE to 510 BCE sees NO WARS for 149 years during this epoch
499 - Persian/Greek wars begin (151 yrs later)
480 - Battle of Himera (19 yrs later)
475 - China warring states (5 yrs later)
460 - 1st Peloponnesian war (15 yrs later)
448 - Persian/Greek Wars end (12 yrs later)
440 - Samian war (8 yrs later)
410 - 2nd Sicilian campaign (30 yrs later)
410 - 2nd Sicilian war
404 - Peloponnesian war (6 yrs later)
399 to 394 - Battle at Thermopoli (5 yrs later)
395 to 387 - Corinthian war
379 to 373 - Boeotian war (8 yrs later)
358 to 336 - Rise of Macedonia wars (18 yrs later)
356 to 346 - 3rd Sacred war (2 yrs later)
343 - Start of Rome/Samnite wars (10 yrs later)
334 - Alexander the Great wars (9 yrs later)
323 to 322 - Lamian war (21 yrs later)
315 - 3rd Sicilian campaign (7 yrs later)
311 to 309 - Babylonian war (4 yrs later)

	305 - Seleucid/Mauryan war (4 yrs later) **290** - End of Rome/Smanite wars (15 yrs later) **281 to 279** - Galls invade the Balkans (9 yrs later) **280 to 275** - Pyrrhic war (1 yr later) **274** - Start of Syrian war (1 yr later) **267 to 261** - Chremonidium war (7 yrs later) **265 to 263** - Kalinga war (4 yrs later) **264** - Start of Punic wars Rome/Carthage (1 yr later) **238** - Parni conquest of Parthia (26 yrs later) **230** - Qin conquest of Han (8 yrs later) **229 to 222** - Cleomenan war (1 yr later) **228** - Qin conquest of Zhao (6 yrs later) **226** - 1st Qin conquest of Yan (2 yrs later) **225** - Qin conquest of Wei (1 yr later) **225** - Qin conquest of Chu **222** - 2nd Qin conquest of Yan (Dai, Wu, and Qi) (3 yrs later) **215 to 168** - Macedonian wars (7 yrs later) **209** - Start of Seleucid/Parthian war (6 yrs later) **205 to 200** - Cretan war (4 yrs later) **200** - End of Syrian wars **195** - Rome/Sparta war (5 yrs later) **191 to 188** - Roma/Syrian war (4 yrs later) **189** - Galation war (1 yr later)
Average interval between wars: **28.8 years**	**167 to 160** - Maccabean revolt (22 yrs later)
Rulership:	**2300 - Meryre Pepi** 2270 - Sumeria falls *(1730 yrs)* 2193 Akkadian Empire falls (141 yrs) 2184 - Merenre Nemtyemsap II Pharaoh 2184-2181 - Neitiqerty Siptah Pharaoh *2181-2169 - 14 Pharaohs @ 9 month average reign per Pharaoh during these disasters* 2055 - Middle Kingdom 1893 - Babylonian Kingdom rises 1600 - Myceneans rise 1600 - Hittites rise 1650 - 2nd Intermediate 1550 - Phoenicians rise 1500 - New Kingdom begins 1499 - Babylonian Kingdom falls (395 yrs) 1487 - Hatshepsut/Tuthmosis III co-Pharaohs 1450- Tuthmosis III Pharaoh dies 1420 - Minoans fall (1280 yrs) 1200 - Philistines rise 1194 - Fall of Troy 1175 - Myceneans fall (425 yrs) 1178 - Hittites fall 900 - Israel & Judah rise

	800 - Greece founded
	753 - Rome founded
	722 - Israel & Judah fall *(178 yrs)*
	600 - Greece falls *(200 yrs)*
	605 - Assyria falls *(1795 yrs)*
	300 - Phoenecians fall *(1250 yrs)*
Religion:	2200 - Minoans initiate goddess worship (Venus!)
	1700 - Rig Vedas created
	@ **1367** - Ahkenaten begins a monotheistic Sun religion
	551 - Confucius born
	440 - Zoroastrianism rises
	150 - Oldest existing fragmentary Hebrew Bible
Texts:	2300 - Epic of Gilgamesh & Enuma Elish written
	2160 - Time of Biblical Abraham
	1900 - Atrahasis written
	1424 - Bharata Battle fought
	1206 to 1187 - Hittite & Ugarit request grain from Egypt during drought
	1000 - Time of David & Solomon ?
	1000 - Atharva Veda written
	508 - Democracy forms in Athens, Greece
Astrology points: 150°, 135°, and 120°	Inconjunct, Sesquiquadrate, and Trine
Genetics/Sociology: States:	1000 bce to 1000 ce - States - 10,000's to 100,000's
	2100 - Ziggurat of Ur built
	2000 - European genetic foundation settles after a major transition
	1917 - Hebrews enter Egypt (Nubkaure Amenemhat II Pharaoh)
	@1800 - Hyksos mentioned in Egypt
	1560 - Hyksos expelled from Egypt
	1487 to 1447 - Hebrew Exodus (40 yrs)
	1200 - First skeleton with metastatic cancer found along the Nile River in modern day Sudan
	580 - Jewish exile
	510 - Jewish return
	800 to 200 - Axial Age (Socrates, Plato, Homer, Lao Tzu, Confuscius)
Diatonic G 432 Scale factor 9: 144° and 126°	144° solar point - 144,000 days = 1 Baktun
	1440° Octahedron sum
	1440 = 60 mins X 24 hrs
	144,000 days sealed Revelations
	1 Mayan Baktun = 144,000 days
	144,000 casing stones Giza pyramid
	126 hr. week = 18 hr X 7 days (24 hr = 168 hrs) = 42 hours added to the week and 6 hours to the day to the present 24 hour day
Geometry:	Octahedron (1440) Octagon, Octagram

Sun Spots:	**1390** - Solar minima **770** - Solar minima (**620** years later) **360** - Solar minima (**410** years later) **720 year average**
Average length of Pharaoh's rule: 1st Intermediate 8 Pharaohs named Horus Middle Kingdom 2nd Intermediate New Kingdom 3rd Intermediate Late Period	2250 - 2230: 10 Pharaohs listed (2 yrs. avg.) ↓Unstable * Turmoil period: 2230 - 2213: (4.25 yrs. avg.) ↑ Unstable 2213 - 2175: (19yrs. avg.) Stable ↑ 2181-2169 - 14 Pharaohs @ 9 month average reign per Pharaoh during the recorded disasters of Sodom, Gomorrah, Bela, Zoar, and Admah 2175 - 2035?: (28 yrs. avg.) ↑ 2134 - 1991 (11.92 yrs. avg.) ↓ 1991 - 1784: (28.875 yrs. avg.) ↑ 4 Pharaohs with "Amen" in their names - Hebrews enter Egypt @ 1917 1784 - 1668: (3.05 yrs. avg.) ↓Unstable 1720 - 1665:(3.44 yrs. avg.) Unstable 1668 - 1560: (13.5 yrs.avg.) ↑ 1665 - 1565: (16.66 yrs. avg.) ↑ 1668 - 1570: (7 yrs. avg.) ↓ Unstable 1570 - 1293: (19.78 yrs avg.) ↑ Stable disaster period 5 Pharaohs with **Amen/Amun** in their names - 3 Pharaohs with **Mosis (Moses)** in their names 1293 - 1195:(13.5 yrs. avg.) ↓ 9 Pharaohs named Ramesses 1185 - 1070: (11:5 yrs. avg.) ↓ 10 Pharaohs named Ramesses 1070 - 656: Upheaval Period 685 - 30: Saite, Persian, Macedonian, and Ptolemaic rule 30 - 495 CE: Roman rule ends, as the Dark Ages begins
Mayan World Sun: 2nd World Sun: Wind Sun (Overthrow) 2184	 Nahui Ehecatl: People become corrupt and are changed into monkeys and Quetzalcoatl (Venus) sends a wind (Evil Wind) to blow them away - Sodom & Gomorrah era disasters Jubilee 10:26, Job 1:19
3rd World Sun: Rain Sun 1487? (Exodus?)	Tlaloc: The next Sun is Tlaloc (?) and his wife Xochiquetzal (?) is stolen by Quetzalcoatl (Venus), so he refuses to send rain and fire is sent from heaven to destroy the 3rd World Gen. 19:24, Exodus 9:24
4th World Sun: Water Sun (Babylonian Exile?) 580	Nahui Atl: Tlaloc's sister Calchiuhtlicue (Saturn) is the next Sun as Tezcatlipoca and Quetzalcoatl (Venus) strike her

	down as Quetzalcoatl (Venus) causes the bones of the dead to rise from the ground
Known Comets Unnamed Comet:	373 BCE 372 BCE

*The **150°** of **2308 BCE** begins the Age of Aries and the **120°** of **148 BCE** begins the Age of Pisces. The Age of Taurus is longed for by mankind, as the tragedies of the Global Flood in **2344 BCE** just **36** years (**1/2** celestial portion) before the Age of Aries begins. This is the reason why the Children of the Exodus craved the Golden Calf (Bull/Taurus) and did not worship the Ram (Aries). They were in the wrong Age, and could not go back, but had to move forward in time and veneration. When the reader begins to approach this with open eyes, it is clear to see the astrotheology that shapes the theology mingled with disastrous events.*

*I broke this portion in to **30** separate celestial portions of **72** years each for **2160** years. This next **4320** years is all too important in the shaping and solidification of our societies, theologies, and wars, up to this point in remembered history.*

2308 BCE - 150° Inconjunct

*__2308 BCE__- The inconjunct symbol in astrology for the **150°** point is curious, as this point ushered in disasters from **2344 BCE** forward, and does seem to be out of junction with the celestial physics. In **2300 BCE** we have the Sahara desert begin formation of the world's first desert a scant **44** years after the Great Global Passover. This is an all too telling link to the parabolic passover made by Venus that has been theorized by Professor Velikovsky and others. Where did all of the grains of sand in the desert come from since the area was not a sea? Answer: Plasma blasted soil! I will elaborate on this later. In **2300 BCE** The Epic of Gilgamesh & Enuma Elish are written in Sumeria. These are some of the earliest epics about a Great Flood, Hero, Divine mission, warring zodiac figures (stars),etc. The **2300 BCE** disaster period sees the Neolithic Period end in China , dates **A1** and **A2** date periods for Unetice culture Europe,   see the collapse of the massive Indus Valley civilization, and sees Meryre Pepi takeover as Pharaoh**.** These are major events and changes within the same calendar year, and points to a global event versus a regional event. Flood fables being documented so close to the event as to be credible in content. An abrupt end to an ancient epoch such as the Neolithic or New Stone Age period ends in China in the same year. The Unetice culture appears in Europe from **2300 BCE** to **1600 BCE** (**1600** is another disaster period), and leaves us with such artifacts as the **"Nebra Sky Disk."** We see Harappa, Mehrgrah, Lothal, and Mohenjo-Daro (Mound of the Dead), all fall as the Indus Valley Civilization completely collapses from an external disaster, as all of these cities are instantly abandoned at this time. **2295 BCE** sees Lugal-zage-si conquer several Sumerian city states. In **2270 BCE** Sumeria falls after **1730** years as a Kingdom, **74** years after the Global Flood, and **30** years after desertification begins. Meryre Pepi takes over as Pharaoh during this period of upheaval. The **30** year period from **2250 BCE** to **2230 BCE** (↓Unstable * **Turmoil period**) sees major instability in rule as **10** Pharaohs are listed for an average reign of **2** years, that has nothing to do* *with infighting, but simply against what they were fighting; disaster, ecological change, climatic changes, parabolic Passovers, meteors, floods, earthquakes, stars, and angry gods in the heavens.*

2236 BCE - 149°

*The instability in reign and resources continue during the period of **2230 BCE - 2213 BCE** as the average reign goes up **4.25** years, but is still an unstable period (↑ Unstable). The 2213 BCE - 2175 BCE period sees a return to stability of reign as the rule averages 19years (Stable ↑). 2200 BCE begins a severe **100** year drought in North Africa that continues the westward spread of desertification. In **2200 BCE** there is a dramatic spike seen in dolomite samples. Dolomite is a sedimentary rock, which means that there was a massive deposition at once, and is typically found in anaerobic conditions in super saline waters (Dead Sea, Red Sea, Black Sea)! The Akkadian Empire falls in **2270 BCE** after 141 years due to the ecological changes.*

*In **2184 BCE** Merenre Nemtyemsap II passes as Pharaoh, and from **2184 BCE** to **2181BCE** Neitiqerty Siptah Pharaoh reigns for **3** three years as the next disaster unfolds in **2184 BCE** causing another upheaval. **2181BCE** to **2169 BCE** sees 14 Pharaohs with a 9 month average reign per Pharaoh during these disasters   **2181BCE** sees the 1st Intermediate period begins with the Biblically remembered tales of Sodom, Gomorrah, Bela, Zoar, and Admah destructions. The rule of the Pharaohs re-stabilizes after the disaster of **21841 BCE** during the period from **2175 BCE** to **2035 BCE** for a **28** year average (↑).*

2nd World Sun: Wind Sun (Overthrow) 2184BCE

***Nahui Ehecatl:** People become corrupt and are changed into monkeys and **Quetzalcoatl** (**Venus**) sends a wind (Evil Wind) to blow them away - Sodom & Gomorrah era disasters*

*Jubilee **10:26**, Job **1:19***

2164 BCE - 148°

***2160 BCE** brings us to the time of the Biblical figure Abram aka Brama (Abraham - Brahma), as their names and deism show similar attributes. We have the first war 49 years after the Great Global Flood Event, and 194 years total with no wars , as in the **2150 BCE** Glutian attacks on Akkad begin the warring anew.*

The late 3rd Intermediate Period rule lowers again due to the conditions of the land from 2134 BCE to 1991BCE down to 11.92 years average (↓). In 2100 BCE the Nile River ceases flowing for 100 to 200 years, as this shows the effects from a planetary passover between the Earth and the Moon. This would disrupt the normal tides that are controlled by the Moon's gravitational/magnetic influence.   The fabled Ziggurat of Ur is built in 2100 BCE, this has been stated to be the much maligned Tower of Babel. The building of this tower in conjunction with the Nile ceasing to flow shows the concern with tracking the mountain in the sky.

2092 BCE - 147°

2049 - Seahenge constructed in Britain   **2047 to 2030** - Ur-Nammu (Lagash)   **2055** - Middle Kingdom

2020 BCE - 146°

Long Island Volcano: NE of New Guinea, Changbaishan Volcano: Eastern China, Liamuiga Volcano: West Indies   Pago Volcano- New Britain Island   27 million people   **2000** - GISP2 Greenland Ice Core Ar-N Isotope Temp reconstruction: snow temp was **30.7C** steady & is **29.9C** now which is colder **(NO Global Warming!)**   **2020** event - dimming Sun, cold, drought, crop failure, famine, with @ 90,000 Egyptian casualties   **2000 to 1000** - Himalayas continued formation, Thar region becomes desert   **2000** - **80%** of Egyptian cities are abandoned at this time   **2000** - Remains found in Turkey of a man who' brain was boiled in his skull   **2000** - First skeletal evidence of leprosy is found in India, just several hundred years after the two devastating passover events of **2344 BCE** and **2184 BCE**.   **2000** - European genetic foundation settles after a major transition   **2000** - Battle of Siddim   1991 - 1784: (28.875 yrs. avg.) ↑

1948 BCE - 145°

In 1940 BCE the Elamites sack the fabled city of **Ur** (**Ur-Anu-s**). The nomadic tribe that will come to be known as "The Children of Israel enter the land of Egypt in **1917 BCE**, as they will spend **430** storied years in the land. The Hebrew people reside under **4** (Nubkaure Amenemhat II Pharaoh) Pharaohs with "**Amen**" in their names. It would be reasonable to assume that when giving thanks to the Lord of the land, that the people would give their thanks for his beneficence by saying **"AMEN,"** before eating being thankful for what they were receiving!   The classic epic called "The **Atrahasis,** is written in **1800 BCE**. The story written in cuneiform tablets survive to this day, and offer one of the earliest written Global Flood accounts. The hero of the classic is **Atrahasis,** also known as **Ziusudra** and **Untnapishtim.** This is another clear example of an earlier tale being plagiarized, with the plagiarizing story (**Noah**) being the accepted version. We see the rise of the Babylonian Kingdom rises in **1893 BCE.**

1876 BCE - 144°

1831 BCE sees Xia China suffer an Earthquake event. The period of **1830 BCE** to **1817 BCE** sees the Amorites gain their independence. The number **144** is important in celestial physics, mathematics, and religion. The 144 relates to the 1440° sum of an octahedron, 1440 minutes in a 24-hour day, 144,000 days in a Mayan Baktun, 144,000 exterior casing stones lined the Great Pyramid of Giza, and in the Book of Revelations there will be 144,000 (DAYS!) sealed for the 12 Tribes of Israel. These understandings and units have been used for geometry, astronomy, and theology.

The *144°* solar point -   *1440°* Octahedron sum   =   *144*,000 days = 1 Baktun

1440 = 60 mins X *24* hrs   *144*,000 days sealed Revelations   1 Mayan Baktun = *144*,000 days

144,000 casing stones Giza pyramid

1804 BCE - 143°

The first mention of a group known as the **Hyksos** appear in Egypt in **1800 BCE**. This same group will wrestle control of Lower Egypt for a short period, before being expelled by **Ahmose I** in **1525 BCE** or **1515 BCE**. For a group to be expelled from a country, means that they had to be allowed in. Who was this group of people known as the **Hyksos**, and where did they go? Historians and educators have recently begun to ask the question if the Hyksos were the **Hebrew** or **Habiru/Apiru** people? This portion of the **2nd Intermediate period** from **1784 BCE** to **1668 BCE**, sees the length of rule drops slightly as the stability begins to slip post disasters *(3.05 yrs. avg ↓Unstable)* and before the onset of the next one to come. **1752 BCE to 1730 BCE** sees Damiq-ilishu defeated in war by Sin-Muballit of Babylon.

1732 BCE - 142°

In **1728 BCE** The famed **Hammurabi (the Kinsman is a healer)** of Babylon rules and sets forth laws and moral codes that are still being echoed in scripture to this day. I could see a link in the name of Hammu-rabi, and that of rabbi. **Rabbi** means *"my master"* or *"great one."* A rabbi could be considered a "healer" to those of his faith, and the Jewish Torah was written during their stay in Babylon in **580 BCE**. The period on **1720 BCE** to **1665 BCE** sees an end to the 2nd Intermediate Period in Egypt, as the length of reign continues to decrease by **3.44** years. The New Kingdom in Egypt begins in **1668 BCE to 1560 BCE** with a **13.5** year average. (↑) as the stability in leadership begins to rise anew, on to the next period of **1665 BCE to 1565 BCE shows a slight rise to 16.66** years average per Pharaoh (↑). The period of **1668 BCE to 1570 BCE** sees stability begin to bottom out as the reign lowers by an average of **7** years per *(↓ Unstable Period).*

1660 BCE - 141°

1650 BCE to 1600 BCE Hattusili & Mursili are defeated, Egypt notes another disaster event in **1628 BCE** with **9 to 10** days of forest fires & floods, this was also recorded as a global event. In **1628 BCE to 1600 BCE** we have the Shang conflict in China, while in **1600 BCE** we have the Hyksos invading Lower Egypt. **1600 BCE** sees the Battle of Mingtiao, as well as the rise of the Myceneans and the Hittites.

1588 BCE - 140°

The **140°** of **1588 BCE** sees the global magnetic field sitting at level **9** and rising. The New Kingdom comes to a close during this period of **1570 BCE to 1293 BCE**, as the length of rule is up to **19.78** years average *(↑ Stable disaster period).* The leadership begin to use the name of **Amen-Amun**, as **5** Pharaohs use this name. This period also sees **3** Pharaohs with **Mosis (Moses)** in their names. The degree closes out in **1550 BCE** we have the rise of the Phoenicians.

1516 BCE - 139°

The Kassites attack Babylon in **1507 BCE**. The bottom begins to fall out in **1500 BCE,** as the fabled city of **Dwarka** sinks into the sea in India, and also in **1500 BCE the Island of Santorini** sinks into the sea in Greece. **1499 BCE** - brings about the Babylonian Kingdom fall after only **395** years. The **1487 BCE** event brings about the Hebrew Exodus from Egypt, as we show no wars **20** years before event as **Hatshepsut** and **Tuthmosis III** reign as co-Pharaoh's, and then there are no wars for **30** years after event (**1** Jubilee planetary passover of **49** years). In **1457 BCE Tuthmosis III** wins the **Battle of Megiddo (Armageddon)** with Canaanite help. **Tuthmosis III (Moses) dies in 1450 BCE,** and did not get to see the **Children of the Exodus enter the Promised Land** as the disaster ends in **1447 BCE**. The post disaster period begins to show the catastrophic effects to the planet from yet another parabolic Passover, as in **1450 BCE** we see the onset of a massive Mediterranean **300** year drought.

3rd World Sun: Rain Sun 1487? (Exodus?)

Tlaloc: The next Sun is Tlaloc (?) and his wife Xochiquetzal (?) is stolen by **Quetzalcoatl (Venus),** so he refuses to send **rain** and **fire** is sent from heaven to destroy the **3rd World**

Gen. 19:24, Exodus 9:24

1444 BCE - 138°

1430 BCE sees the Kaska invasion of Hatti start. In **1424 BCE** the much written of **Bharata Battle** fought on the land and in the skies of India. **1420 BCE** ushers in the fall of the Minoan after **1280** years. **1400 BCE** sees the battle for the city of Ai, and the Battle of the 10 Kings as well. We close out the degree in **1390 BCE** with a solar minima cold period.

1372 BCE - 137°

Egyptian records show a 1370 BCE event with **50** days of **dimming Sun**, **2** years of dust in the skies, **7** years of famine: **3** phases, dimming Sun, cold, drought, crop failure, famine, **950,000** global casualties. This is yet another similar account to that of **Joseph/Zaphnath Paaneah (One Who Sees Hidden Things aka Magician)** in the **Torah** and **Bibles**. In **1350 BCE** the Kaska invasions of Hatti end.

1300 BCE - 136°

The Late 3rd Intermediate Period spans **1293 BCE** to **1195 BCE,** and sees a continued downward spiral in length of leadership to **13.5** years average (↓). There are **9** Pharaohs named Ramesses during this era as in **1279 BCE** to **1213 BCE** Ramesses II wages a Near East campaign. In **1274 BCE** we have the Egyptian Battle of Kadesh. We get the often told tale of the Trojan War waged from **1260 BCE to 1240 BCE** as the drought begun **190** years earlier in **1450 BCE** brings the Mediterranean area explodes in a rage over resources. In **1232 BCE to 1225BCE** we get Tukulti-Ninurta 1 Assyrian asserting supremacy over Babylon.

1228 BCE - 135° Sesquiquadrate

In **1206BCE to 1187 BCE** there are records of Hittite and Ugarit request for grain from Egyptian storehouses during a drought period.

In **2014 CE** researchers announced the findings of the first known skeleton with metastatic cancer located along the Nile River in modern day Sudan from **1200 BCE**. This is a major link to the degradation of the ecosystem from extra-planetary influences that fundamentally changed the human DNA, bringing *with it genetic defects and diseases that still plague us to this day. In **1200 BCE** we see the Philistines rise during this period of upheaval, as the Kurukshetra war starts in **1200 BCE** as well. In **1194 BCE** the fabled Fall of Troy takes place, as we see a long period of wars begin in the Mediterranean and surrounding regions. The Hittite kingdom falls in **1178 BCE** after only **422** years, and the Myceneans fall in **1175 BCE** after only **425** years in the limelight. The Egyptian records show an **1159 BCE** event of **40** and **40** days, for **80** days total of torrential rain, cold, floods, forest fires, and **5.8** million global casualties: This event comes on the heels of the Dardanus Flood (after **1194** event) that claimed **3.8** million global casualties, with flooding **18'** of water.*

*The portion of the **3rd Intermediate Period** from **1185 BCE to 1070 BCE**, sees the reign of the Pharaoh continue to decrease to **11.5** years. average (↓). There are **10** Pharaohs named Ramesses (Aries/Aryan Age) during this portion, but the **3,000** years plus of being the pinnacle is about to end due to foreign invaders beginning to rise in other regions. The collapse of Egypt from internal strife is incorrect, as the external disasters weakened the high point of human society known thus far.*

<u>1156 BCE - 134°</u>

*In **1150 BCE** the **300** hundred year drought begun in **1450 BCE** in the Mediterranean ends. We see the direct relationship between the **1500 BCE** and **1487 BCE** events, as it begins to show the effects from these disastrous planetary passovers.*

<u>1084 BCE - 133°</u>

*This is the last true period for Egyptian Rule from **1070 BCE to 656 BCE**, as after this upheaval period they will be ruled by the Persians, Macedonians, Ptolemy's, and the Romans. In **1046 BCE** the Battle of Muye in China is waged.*

<u>1012 BCE - 132°</u>

*The **132°** has the Earth's global magnetic field rising to **11**, as this is the highest level recorded and speaks to an external source for the rapid increase. In **1000 BCE** we have the Seige of Jebus, the time of the Biblical of **David & Solomon**, and the Hindu text the **Atharva Veda** is written. In **1000 BCE** smallpox is noted in the Egyptian records. The period of **1000 BCE** to **1000 CE** sees humanity groups in to states of **10,000** to **100,000** people.*

<u>940 BCE - 131°</u>

*The global population continues the steady increase up to **100** million people, as in **900 BCE** we have the rise of Israel & Judah.*

<u>868 BCE - 130°</u>

*We have in **800 BCE** the founding of Greece, as **800 BCE to 200 BCE** is considered the Axial Age for all of the philosophy that sprouted up during this period. There was the rise of philosophers such as; Socrates,*

Plato, Homer, Lao Tzu, and Confucius. All of the writings and philosophical systems of the time seem to be retellings of Egyptian understandings.

796 BCE - 129°

*In **770 BCE** we have a solar minima cold period, as in **753 BCE** Rome is founded, and also in **740 BCE** we have the start of the **1st** Messenian war.*

724 BCE - 128°

*In **722 BCE** has the fall of Israel & Judah after only **178** years, which is less that 3 degrees/celestial portions. **720 BCE** brings an end to the 1st Messenian war, in **710** the Lelantine war starts, and in **701 BCE** Sennacherib's campaigns are waged. The Egyptian rule of their country comes to a crashing end from **685 BCE to 30 BCE**, as the Saite, Persian, Macedonian, and Ptolemaic rule takes over their land. In **685 BC the 2nd** Messenian war begins, and in **668 BCE** the **2nd** Messenian war ends.*

652 BCE - 127°

*In **650 BCE** the Lelantine war ends after **60** years. In **605 BCE** the mighty Assyrian empire falls after **1795** years. Another round of disasters brings about civil wars that allows the Scythians and Cimmerians to overtake the Assyrians. We have the fall of Greece after only **200** years in **600 BCE.***

580 BCE - 126°

*The **126°** is an important one in history, as in **580 BCE** what has become known as the " **Jewish Exile,"** or the **"Babylonian Captivity,"** occurs for the Children of Israel. I have stated in other works, and will go into greater detail later, but I believe this move by the Babylonians to be a forced relocation. The Babylonian in earlier times were also known as the Chaldean (Abram's home) who were noted astronomers, and would have known the parabolic path of the disaster to come. In **551 BCE** the wise Confucius is born. The **520 BCE NOAA** Dunde ice cores from **1500** Year d**180**, shows dust, anion, and accumulation data shows **abrupt change**, and corresponds **directly** to **structural changes in civilizations**. This correlation is not by accident, but shows that the cause of the **Exile/Captivity** was based on **external disaster**. The close of the **126°** in **510 BCE** brings a return **70** years later of the Jewish faithful return, as the Babylonians return **100%** of the Children of Israel's gold and silver from the temple.*

126 hr. week = 18 hr X 7 days (24 hr = 168 hrs) = 42 hours added to the week and 6 hours to the day to the present 24 hour day.

4th World Sun: Water Sun (Babylonian Exile 580 BCE)

Nahui Atl: *Tlaloc's sister **Calchiuhtlicue** (Saturn) is the next **Sun** as **Tezcatlipoca** and **Quetzalcoatl** (Venus) strike her down as **Quetzalcoatl** (Venus) causes the **bones** of the **dead** to **rise** from the **ground***

508 BCE - 125°

In 508 BCE democracy forms in Athens, Greece. Democracy is Greek for "rule of the people," and has come to be known as the system of American government. Demo in modern use has come to mean a test or example, and shows that **demo-cracy** (demo-crazy)is a test that may not be working! **NOAA** Ice core samples from **500 BCE** the WAIS Divide Ice Core 1500 Year elevated sulfate & nitrogen isotope data. In **500 BCE** the Subboreal period ends, and the Subatlantic period begins, as we see the Persian/Greek wars begin in **499 BCE**.

In **480 BCE** the Battle of Himera is fought, in **475 BCE** in China the warring states engage in war, in **464 BCE** in Sparta Greece a massive earthquake event occurs, the **1st** Peloponnesian war is fought in **460 BCE**. and in **448 BCE** the Persian/Greek Wars ends. The Samian war is fought in **440 BCE**, as in the same year Zoroastrianism rises.

436 BCE - 124°

Egyptian records show a **430 BCE** event of **13** days of forest fires, flooding, rain, and **830,000** local casualties. In **410 BCE the 2nd** Sicilian campaign and the **2nd** Sicilian wars are fought. The Mediterranean continues to be the theatre for wars as in **404 BCE** the Peloponnesian war is wage, we see in **399 BCE to 394 BCE** the Battle at Thermopoli, from **395 BCE to 387 BCE** we have the Corinthian war, and finally from **379 BCE to 373 BCE** we have the Boeotian war.

364 BCE - 123°

360 BCE begins with a solar minima cold period. **From 358 BCE to 336 BCE** we see the rise of the Macedonia wars, from **356 BCE to 346 BCE** the **3rd** Sacred war is waged, **343 BCE** we have the start of the Rome/Samnite wars, in **334 BCE** Alexander the Great begins to wage wars. In **323 BCE to 322 BCE** the Lamian war is waged, in **315 BCE** the **3rd** Sicilian campaign unfolds, from **311 BCE to 309 BCE** the Babylonian war is fought, and in **305 BCE the** Seleucid/Mauryan war sees the continuation of warring in the Mediterranean. The mighty sailing power the Phoenecians fall after **1250** years in **300 BCE.**

292 BCE - 122°

290 BCE brings the end of the Rome/Samanite wars, as from **281 BCE to 279 BCE** sees the Galls invade the Balkans, **280 BCE to 275 BCE** sees the Pyrrhic war waged, **274 BCE** has the start of the Syrian war, **267 BCE to 261 BCE** has the Chremonidium war, from **265 BCE to 263 BCE** the Kalinga war rages, in **264 BCE** the start of the Punic wars between Rome and Carthage, in **238 BCE** has the Parni conquest of Parthia, **230 BCE** has the Qin conquest of Han **229 to 222** - Cleomenan war **228** - Qin conquest of Zhao **226** - 1st Qin conquest of Yan **225** - Qin conquest of Wei **225** - Qin conquest of Chu **222** - 2nd Qin conquest of Yan (Dai, Wu, and Qi) **226** - Rhodes Greece EQ

220 BCE - 121°

215 to 168 - Macedonian wars **209** - Start of Seleucid/Parthian war **207** event - 8 days of forests fires, floods, and rain, with 530,000 local casualties **205 to 200** - Cretan war **200** - End of Syrian wars

195 - Rome/Sparta war   191 to 188 - Roma/Syrian war   189 - Galation war   167 to 160 - Maccabean revolt   150 - Oldest existing fragmentary Hebrew Bible

148 BCE - 120° Trine

126 hr. week = 18 hr X 7 days (24 hr = 168 hrs) = 42 hours added to the week and 6 hours to the day to the present 24 hour day

Geometry: Octahedron (Platonic Solid - Air) and Octagon

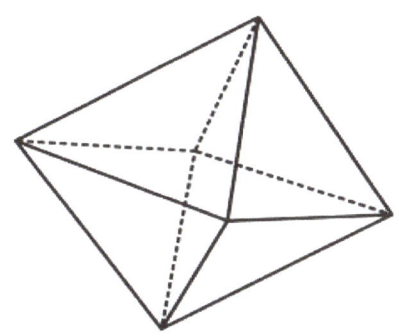

Octahedron sum = 1440°

Star of Lakshmi / Rub el-hzib

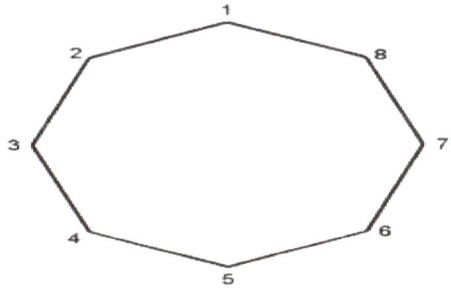

Octagon sum = 1440°

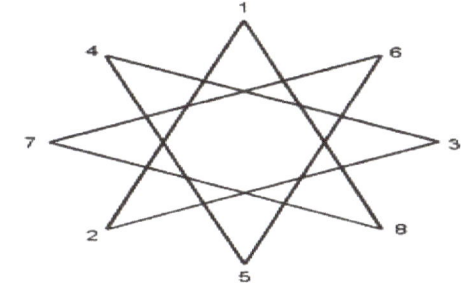

Octagram is derived from an octagon

Astrology: Age of Aries

Aries 150° to Pisces 120°

Aries the Ram symbol

Mars is the planetary ruler of Aries

120° to 90° Portion of the Heavens (9/12th)

120° to 90° 148 BCE to 2012 CE = 2160 years	Age of Pisces to Age of Aquarius
Scientific Epoch: Subatlantic	225 ce - Sub-Atlantic period (increased rainfall) 1250 to 1850 - Little Ice Age
Solfeggio Frequencies: 147/174 to 258	Varying range along the scale
Solfeggio Music Note:	
Volcanic Eruptions:	100 BCE - Mt. Okmok (150 YL) 50 BCE - Apoyeque (50 YL) 50 BCE - Ambrym 79 CE- Vesuvius Volcano (Pompeii & Herculaneum) Taupo Volcano - North Island New Zealand (129 YL) 230 - Taupo (151 YL) 240 - Ksudach volcano (10 YL) 416 - Krakatoa (176 YL) 450 - Lake Ilopango (34 YL) 540 - Rabaul Caldera (90 YL) 700 - Mt. Churchill (160 YL) 710 - Pago (10 YL) 800 - Dakataua (90 YL) 930 - Ceboruco (130 YL) 934 to 940 - Katla (4 YL) 969 - Mt. Baekdu (29 YL) 1258 - Mt. Rinjani (289 YL) 1280 - Quilota (22 YL) 1450 - Aniakchak Volcano (170 YL) 1452 - Kuwae Volcano (2 YL) 1471 - Sakurajima Volcano (19 YL) 1477 - Bardarbunga Volcano (6 YL) 1480 and 1482 - Mount St. Helen Volcano (3 and 2 YL) 1540 - Mount St. Helen Volcano (58 YL) 1580 - Billy Mitchell Volcano (40 YL) 1586 - Kelut Volcano (6 YL) 1593 - Raung Volcano (7 YL) 1600 - Huaynaputina Volcano (7 YL) 1640 - Kamaga-Take Volcano (40 YL) 1641 - Parker Volcano (1 YL) 1660 - Long Island Volcano (19 YL) 1663 - Usu Volcano (3 YL) 1667 - Tarumai Volcano (4 YL) 1673 - Gamkonora Volcano (7 YL) 1680 - Tongkoko Volcano (7 YL) 1680 - Krakatoa Volcano 1739 - Tarumai Volcano (59 YL) 1755 - Katla Volcano (16 YL) 1783 - Laki Volcano(23 YL)

	1815 - Tambora Volcano (32 YL)
	1822 - Galunggung Volcano (7 YL)
	1835 - Cosiguina Volcano (13 YL)
	1854 - Sheveluch Volcano (19 YL)
	1875 - Askja Volcano (21 YL)
	1875 - Tarawera Volcano
	1883 - Krakatau Volcano (8 YL)
	1902 - Santa Maria Volcano (19 YL)
	1907 - Ksudach Volcano (5 YL)
	1911 - Katmai Volcano (4 YL)
	1932 - Cerro Azul Volcano (21 YL)
	1956 - Bezymianny Volcano (24 YL)
	1980 - Mount St. Helens Volcano (24 YL)
Major Eruption Average: **40.75 Years**	1991 - Mt. Piatubo (11 YL)
Earthquakes:	60 BCE- Portugal & Galicia EQ
	17 CE - Asia Minor Lydia EQ (77 YL)
	62 - Naples/Pompeii EQ (45 YL)
	110 - Yunnan China EQ (48 YL)
	115 - Antioch EQ (5 YL)
	300 - New Madrid Earthquake (185 YL)
	365 - Crete Greece EQ (65 YL)
	382 - Cape St. Vincent EQ (17 YL)
	526 - Antioch Turkey EQ (144 YL)
	551 - Beirut, Turkey, Tripoli EQ (25 YL)
	700- Mt. Edziza (149 YL)
	749 - Levant Region EQ (49 YL)
	847 - Damascus Syria EQ (102 YL)
	856 - Corinth Greece EQ (9 YL)
	856 - Qumis Iran EQ
	869 - Sendai Japan EQ (13 YL)
	893 - Divin Armenia EQ (24 YL)
	893 - Ardabil Iran EQ
	900 - New Madrid Earthquake (7 YL)
	1042 - Baalbek, Palmyra, Syria EQ (142 YL)
	1068 - Near East EQ (26 YL)
	1138 - Aleppo Syria EQ (70 YL)
	1157 - Hama Syria EQ (19 YL)
	1169 - Sicily Italy EQ (12 YL)
	1170 - Eastern Meditteranean EQ (1 YL)
	1201/1202 - Eastern Mediterranean EQ (31 YL)
	1222 - Cyprus Greece EQ (20 YL)
	1268 - Cilicia, Anatolia EQ (46 YL)
	1290 - Chihli China EQ (22 YL)
	1293 - Kamakura Japan EQ (3 YL)
	1303 - Crete Greece EQ (10 YL)
	1348 - Friuli, Venice, Rome EQ (45 YL)
	1356 - Basel Switzerland (8 YL)
	1384 - Canterbury England EQ (28 YL)

	1428 - Catalonia EQ (Spain) (54 YL)
1450 - New Madrid Earthquake (22 YL)
1453 - Kuwae Volcano   (3 YL)
1481 - Rhodes Greece EQ (29 YL)
1498 - Honshu Japan EQ (17 YL)
1509 - Istanbul Turkey EQ (11 YL)
1531 - Lisbon Portugal EQ (22 YL)
1556 - Shaanxi China EQ   (25 YL)
1570 - Ferrara Italy EQ
1575 - Valdivia Chile EQ (24 YL)
1600 - Huaynaputina Volcano (30 YL)
1604 - Arica Chile EQ   (4 YL)
1605 - Shikoku & Honshu Japan EQ   (1 YL)
1605 - Qiongshan& Hainan China EQ
1663 - Quebec Canada EQ   (2 YL)
1667 - Dubrovnik Croatia EQ (4 YL)
1667 - Shamakhi Azerbaijan EQ
1668 - Anatolia Turkey EQ (1 YL)
1687 - Lima Peru EQ   (19 YL)
1692 - Salta Province Argentina EQ (5 YL)
1692 - Port Royal Jamaica EQ
1693 - Catania Province Sicily EQ (1 YL)
1694 - Irpinia Italy EQ   (1 YL)
1700 - Cascadia Zone EQ (6 YL)
1703 - Norcia Italy EQ   (3 YL)
1703 - L'Aquil Italy EQ
1703 - Kanto Japan EQ
1707 - Japan EQ   (4 YL)
1727 - Tabriz Iran EQ (20 YL)
1730 - Beijing China EQ (3 YL)
1730 - Kamchatka Russia EQ
1730 - Valparaiso Chile EQ
1746 - Lima/Callao Peru EQ (16 YL)
1751 - Concepcion Chile EQ (5 YL)
1755 - Northern Persia EQ   (4 YL)
1755 - Boston Massachusetts EQ
1755 - Lisbon Portugal EQ
1759 - Eastern Mediterranean EQ (4 YL)
1762 - Eastern Bay of Bengal EQ   (3 YL)
1766 - St. Joseph, Trinidad, Tobago EQ (4 YL)
1770 - Port Au-Prince Haiti EQ   (4 YL)
1773 - Guatemala EQ (3 YL)
1780 - Iran EQ (7 YL)
1783 - Calabria Italy EQ (3 YL)
1786 - Sichuan China EQ (3 YL)
1797 - Quito Ecuador & Cuzco Peru EQ (11 YL)
1800 - San Diego EQ   (3 YL)
1833 - Sumatra Indonesia EQ (33 YL)

	1868 - Arica Chile EQ (25 YL) 1906 - San Francisco EQ (38 YL) 1906 - Ecuador & Colombia EQ 1952 - Kamchatka Russia EQ (46 YL) 1960 - Valdivia Chile EQ (8 YL) 1964 - Prince William Sound EQ (4 YL) 1965 - Rat Island Alaska EQ (1 YL) 2004 - Sumatra Indonesia EQ (39 YL) 2010 - Maule Chile EQ (6 YL) 2010 - Haiti EQ
Earthquake Average: 21.57 Years	2010 - Chile, EQ
Geomagnetic Field:	11 (4 BCE) ≤11 (716 CE) ≤11 (1508 CE) ≤10 (1868 CE) 9 (2012)
Global Population:	1804 - 1b 1927 - 2b 1960 - 3b 1974 - 4b 1987 - 5b 1999 - 6b **2011 - 7 billion people**
Dendrochronology:	774 to 775 - High Levels of Carbon-14 in tree rings in Japan (gamma ray?)
NOAA Ice Core:	172 - EPICA Dronning Maud Land: Volcanic sulphate increase 997 - East Rongbuk Glacier Mt. Everest: a decrease in marine and increase in continental air masses since 1400 1450 - Dasauopu Ice Core Nepal: chloride concentrations doubled 1500 - Lewis Glacier - Microparticle Data 1650 - East Rongbuk Glacier 350 year trace element data
Disasters:	44 BCE event - 2 (months) 7 days 2 years - forest fires, dust, cold, drought, crop failure, famine, 500,000 casualties locally: "Caesar's Comet" 235 to 284 CE - Crisis of the 3rd century affects Rome 416 CE event - 1 year of dust, cold, famine, crop failure, drought, 250,000 local casualties: Eruption of Krakatau - Islands of Java & Sumatra are separated 450 - Malaria epidemic in Italy 536/540 event - Dark Ages onset, 21 months of dust, diminished sunlight, dust, drought, cold, famine, crop failure, 2.9 million casualties globally 1054 - A Supernova creates the Crab Nebula 1099 - Hodh Ech Chargui & Hodh El Gharbi regions of Mauritania become deserts 1345 CE - The Black Death/Bubonic plague spreads across Europe killing ≥ 100 million people **1500 - 0.5 Kiloyear event** 1601 - Coldest year in six century after Huaynaputina erupts in 1600 causing famines 1770 - India's Monsoons fail causing widespread famine 1816 - Year Without A Summer," after the eruption of Tambora in 1815

Wars:	146 bce - End of Punic wars between Carthage/Rome (14 yrs later)
	138 to 111 - Han campaign against the Minuye (8 yrs later)
	135 - Start of Roman Servile wars (3 yrs later)
	133 to 89 - Han/Xiongnu war (2 yrs later)
	122 to 105 - Jugurthine war (11 yrs later)
	113 to 101 - Cimbrian war (8 yrs later)
	109 to 108 - Gojoseon/Han war (8 yrs later)
	111 - Han/Nanyue war (3 yrs later)
	109 - Han campaign against Dian (2 yrs later)
	91 to 88 - Social wars Rome (18 yrs later)
	89 to 85 - 1st Mithridatic war (1 yr later)
	88 - End of Seleucid/Parthian wars (3 yrs later)
	88 to 87 - Sullas 1st civil war
	83 to 82 - 2nd Mithridatic war (4 yrs later)
	82 to 81 - Sulla's 2nd civil war
	74 to 63 - 3rd Mithridatic war (7 yrs later)
	71 - End of Roman Servile wars (8 yrs later)
	65 - Pompey's Georgian campaign (8 yrs later)
	63 - Pompey captures Jerusalem (2 yrs later)
	58 to 50 - Julius Caesar's Gallic wars (5 yrs later)
	55 to 54 - Julius Caesar's invasion of Britian (5 yrs later)
	53 to 51 - Parthian war (Marcus Licinius Crassus) (1 yr later)
	49 to 45 - Caesar's civil war (2 yrs later)
	44 to 30 - Roman civil wars (Post Caesarian, Liberator's civil war, Sicilian revolt, Fulvia's civil war) (1 yr later)
	40 to 33 - Anthony's Parthian war (4 yrs later)
	34 to 22 BCE - Chinese war (1 yr later)
	No noted wars 22 years before the noted time of Jesus Christ (JC) and the first war is 43 years after the CE Common Era for a total of 65 years free of documented wars
	43 to 96 CE - Roman conquest of Britian (65 yrs later)
	58 to 63 - Roman Parthian war (15 yrs later)
	60 to 61 - Boudica's uprising (2 yrs later)
	66 to 73 - 1st Roman/Jewish war (5 yrs later)
	70 - Jewish Temple destroyed (4 yrs later)
	101 to 102 - 1st Dacian war (31 yrs later)
	105 to 106 - 2nd Dacian war (3 yrs later)
	115 to 117 - Kitos war (9 yrs later)
	132 to 136 - Bar Kokhba Revolt (15 yrs later)
	161 to 166 - Roman Parthian war (24 yrs later)
	166 to 180 - Marcomannic wars
	184 to 205 - Yellow Turban Rebellion (4 yrs later)
	190 to 191 - Campaign against Dong Zhuo (6 yrs later)
	194 to 199 - Sun Ce's conquest of Jiandong (3 yrs later)

216 - Caracalla's Parthian war   (17 yrs later)
225 - Zhuge Liang's Southern campaign (9 yrs later)
228 to 234 - Zhuge Liang's Northern campaigns (3 yrs later)
247 to 262 - Jiang Wei's Northern campaigns (13 yrs later)
263 - Wei's conquest of Shu   (1 yr later)
279 to 280 - Jin conquers Wu (16 yrs later)
291 to 306 - Eight Princes war (11 yrs later)
376 to 382 - Gothic war   (70 yrs later)
416 - Krakatau erupts creating Java & Sumatra as Islands
421 to 422 - Roman/Sasanian war   (43 yrs later)
(One war noted 6yr after event - No wars until 72 years later)
502 to 506 - Anastasian war (82 yrs later)
526 to 532 - Iberian war (20 yrs later)
527 - Iwai rebellion (1 yr later)
533 to 534 - Vandalic war (6 yrs later)
534 to 537 - War against the Moors
534 to 554 - Gothic war (3 yrs later)
541 to 562 - Lazic war (7 yrs later)
572 to 591 - Byzantine-Sasanian war (10 yrs later)
588 - First Perso-Turkic war (3 yrs later)
598 to 614 - Goguryeo-Sui wars (10 yrs later)
600 - Frisnian-Frankish wars start (2 yrs later)
602 to 628 - Byzantine-Sasanian war   (2 yrs later)
619 - Second Perso-Turkish war (9 yrs later)
627 to 629 - Third Perso-Turkish war (8 yrs later)
627 to 630 - Taizong's campaign against Eastern Tujue
632 to 633 - Ridda wars (2 yrs later)
633 to 644 - Muslim conquest of Persia
634 - Start of Byzantine-Arab wars (1 yr later)
640 to 657 - Tang's campaign against Western Turks (6 yrs later)
640 to 648 - Taizong's campaign against Xiyu states
640 - Tang campaign Karakhoja
644 to 648 - Tang campaign against Karahasar (4 yrs later)
644 to 688 - Goguryeo-Tang war
645 to 646 - Taizong's campaign against Xueyantuo (1 yr later)
648 - Tang campaign against Kucha (2 yrs later)
650 - Start of Khazar-Arab wars (2 yrs later)
656 to 661 - First Fitna   (5 yrs later)
657 - Tang conquest of Western Turks
670 to 676 - Silla-Tang wars (1 yr later)
672 - 672 - Jinshin war (2 yrs later)
680 - Start of Byzantine-Bulgarian wars (8 yrs later)

711 to 718 - Umayyad conquest of Hispania (31 yrs later)
715 to 718 - Frankish Civil War (3 yrs later)
717 to 718 - Arab siege of Constantinople (2 yrs later)
732 - Battle of Tours (14 yrs later)
735 to 737 - Marwin ibn Muhammad invasion of Georgia (3 yrs later)
751 - Battle of Talas (14 yrs later)
755 to 763 - An Lushan Rebellion (4 yrs later)
758 - End of Khazar-Arab wars (3 yrs later)
772 - Start of Saxon wars (14 yrs later)
793 - Frisnian-Frankish wars end (21 yrs later)
804 - End of Saxon wars (11 yrs later)
839 - Start of Bulgarian-Serbian wars (35 yrs later)
854 - Start of Croatian-Bulgarian wars (15 yrs later)
869 to 883 - Zanj Rebellion (15 yrs later)
894 - Start of Bulgarian-Hungarian wars (11 yrs later)
941 - Rus'-Byzantine war
955 - Battle of Lechfield (14 yrs later)
977 to 978 - War of the Three Henries (22 yrs later)
993 - First Goryeo-Khitan war (15 yrs later)
999 - Battle of Svolder (6 yrs later)
1000 - End of Croatian-Bulgarian wars (1 yr later)
1003 - End of Bulgarian-Hungarian wars (3 yrs later)
1066 - Norman conquest of England (63 yrs later)
1096 - First Holy Crusade (30 yrs later)
1101 - Holy Crusade of 1101 (5 yrs later)
1145 to 1149 - Second Holy Crusade (44 YL)
1147 to 1242 - Northern Holy Crusades (2 YL)
1169 to 1175 - Norman Invasion of Ireland (27 YL)
1180 - End of Byzantine-Arab wars (5 YL)
1189 to 1192 - Third Holy Crusade (9 YL)
1202 to 1204 - Fourth Holy Crusade (10 YL)
1202 to 1214 - Anglo/French War
1206 to 1337 - Mongol Conquests (4 YL)
1208 to 1227 - Livonian Holy Crusade (2 YL)
1213 to 1221 - Fifth Holy Crusade (5 YL)
1228 - Sixth Holy Crusade (15 YL)
1248 to 1254 - Seventh Holy Crusade (20 YL)
1270 - Eigth Holy Crusade (16 YL)
1271 to 1272 - Ninth Holy Crusade (1 YL)
1330 - End of Bulgarian-Serbian wars (58 YL)
1337 - Start of Hundred Years War (7 YL)
1355 - End of Byzantine-Bulgarian wars (18 YL)
1375 to 1378 - War of the Eight Saints (20 YL)
1419 to 1434 - Hussite Wars (41 YL)
1453 - End of Hundred Years War (19 YL)
1453 - Fall of Constantinople
1467 - War of the Priests (14 YL)

1482 to 1484 - War of Ferrara (15 YL)
1494 to 1498 - Italian War (10 YL)
1508 to 1516 - War of the League of Cambrai (10 YL)
1521 to 1526 - Italian War (6 YL)
1527 to 1697 - Spanish Conquest of Yucatan (1 YL)
1527 to 1528 - Hungarian Campaign (30 YL)
1530 to 1552 - Little War in Hungary (2 YL)
1536 to 1538 - Italian War (6 YL)
1542 to 1546 - Italian War (6 YL)
1551 to 1559 - Italian War (6 YL)
1562 to 1598 - French Wars of Religion (13 YL)
1571 - Russo/Crimean War (12 YL)
1592 to 1598 - Japanese invasions of Korea (21 YL)
1635 to 1659 - French/Spanish War (37 YL)
1639 - First Bishops' War (4 YL)
1640 - Second Bishops' War (1 YL)
1641 to 1644 - First War of Castro (1 YL)
1644 to 1651 - Scottish War of the Three Kingdoms
1649 - Second War of Castro (5 YL)
1683 to 1699 - Great Turkish War (34 YL)
1683 to 1684 - War of the Reunions
1701 to 1714 - War of the Spanish Succession (17 YL)
1718 to 1720 - War of the Quadruple Alliance (4 YL)
1754 to 1763 - French/Indian War (34 YL)
1775 to 1783 - American Revolutionary War (12 YL)
1810 - U.S. Occupation of West Florida (27 YL)
1810 to 1821 - Mexican War of Independence
1812 to 1815 - War of 1812 (2 YL)
1835 to 1836 - Texas Revolution (20 YL)
1838 - Mormon War (2 YL)
1839 to 1842 - First Opium War (1 YL)
1846 to 1848 - Mexican/American War (4 YL)
1856 to 1860 - Second Opium War (8 YL)
1861 to 1865 - American Civil War (1 YL)
1899 to 1901 - Boxer Rebellion (34 YL)
1912 - Negro Rebellion (11 YL)
1914 to 1919 - World War I (2 YL)
1917 to 1923 - Russian Civil War (3 YL)
1936 to 1939 - Arab Revolt in Palestine (13 YL)
1936 to 1939 - Spanish Civil War
1939 to 1945 - World War II (3 YL)
1944 to 1947 - Jewish insurgency in Palestine (1 YL)
1948 to 1949 - Arab/Israeli War (1 YL)
1950 to 1953 - Korean War (1 YL)
1956 to 1975 - Vietnam War (3 YL)
1967 - Six Day War (8 YL)
1973 - Yom-Kippur War (7 YL)
1979 to 1989 - Soviet/Afghanistan War (6 YL)

	1980 to 1988 - Iran/Iraq War (1 YL)
	1990 - Invasion of Kuwait (2 YL)
	1990 to 1991 Persian Gulf War
	1992 to 1995 - Bosnian War (1 YL)
	1996 to 2001 - Afghan Civil War (1 YL)
	2001 to present - War in Afghanistan
	2003 to 2011 - Iraq War (2 YL)
Average Interval Between Wars: **10.27 Years**	2007 - Operation Enduring Freedom (4 YL)
Rulership:	30 - 495 CE: Roman rule ends as the Dark Ages begin
	Genghis Khan, Great Britain, France, Russia, Germany, United States, and others
Religion:	@ 50 CE - Christianity founded
	325 - Council of Nicea (275 YL)
	350 - Oldest surviving Septuagint (25 YL)
	380 - Nicene Christianity named religion of Roman empire (30 YL)
	393 - Synod of Hippo approves early Christian canon (13 YL)
	570 - Prophet Muhammad born (177 YL)
	639 - Prophet Muhammad dies (69 YL)
	1054 - The Great Schism (415 YL)
	1320 - Pope John Paul XXII enacts witchcraft doctrines (266 YL)
	1484 - Pope Innocent VIII begins European witch hunt (164 YL)
	1545 - 1563 Council of Trent (61 YL)
	1830 - Mormons or Latter Day Saints are formed (285 YL)
	1875 - Theosophical Society is founded by Madam Helena Blavatsky (45 YL)
	1904 - Thelema founded (29 YL)
	1930's - Rastafari movement (26 YL)
	1930's - Nation of Islam founded
	1952 - Scientology created by SciFi writer L. Ron Hubbard (22 YL)
	1966 - Anton Szandor LaVey starts the Church of Satan (24 YL)
	1973 - Raelian movement founded (7 YL)
Texts:	350 - Talmud written?
	610 - Koran written
	1611 - King James Bible released
Genetics/Sociology Empires:	1000 ce to present - Empires: 100,000's to 1,000,000's
	49 - Julius Caesar (JC) dies
	4 - Jesus Christ (JC) born
	2 - King Herod dies
	Texts during this period - Zoroaster - Buddha - Revelations? - Nag Hammadi - Zohar - Popul Vuh - Jewish Talmud - Babylonian Talmud

Astrology Point: 120° and 90°	Trine (120) & Square (90)
Diatonic G 432 Scale factor 9: 126°	126 hr. week = 18 hr X 7 days (24 hr = 168 hrs) = 42 hours added to the week and 6 hours to the day to the present 24 hour day
Geometry: none	
Sun Spots:	1040 to 1080 CE -Oort minimum (Medieval Warm Period) 1100 to 1250 - Medieval maximum (Medieval Warm Period) 1280 to 1350 - Wolf minimum 1450 to 1550 - Sporer minimum 1645 to 1715 - Maunder minimum 1790 to 1820 - Daulton minimum 1900 to present - Modern maximum **Average: 308.57 years**
Average length of Pharaoh's rule:	30 - 495 CE: Roman rule ends, as the Dark Ages begins
Mayan World Sun: 5th World Sun: Earthquake Sun 416 CE? The present Sun that exists in the sky	*Nanahuatzin:* Nanahuatzin is chosen as the 4th World Sun, as Tecuciztecatl jumps in as well and the brightness causes the Gods to throw a sackcloth over the Moon
Known Comets Halley's Comet: Caesar's Comet (C/-43K1): Halley's Comet: Great Comet: Donati's Comet: Great Comet: Great Daylight Comet: Halley's Comet: Skjellerup-Maristany Comet: Arend-Roland Comet: Seki-Lanes Comet:	 87 BCE 44 BCE (43 YL) 12 BCE (32 YL) 531 CE (543 YL) 536 CE (5 YL) 540 CE * Series of 3 comets ushers in the Dark Ages (4 YL) 1066 CE (526 YL) 1106 CE (50 YL) 1264 CE (158 YL) 1402 CE (138 YL) 1556 CE (154 YL) 1577 CE (21 YL) 1680 CE (103 YL) 1744 CE (64 YL) 1811 CE (67 YL) 1823 CE (12 YL) 1825 CE (2 YL) 1843 CE (18 YL) 1858 CE (15 YL) 1861 CE (3 YL) 1882 CE (1 YL) 1910 CE (28 YL) 1910 CE 1927 CE (17 YL) 1957 CE (30 YL) 1962 CE (5 YL)

Ikeya-Seski Comet:	1965 CE (3 YL)
Comet West:	1976 CE (11 YL)
Hyakutake Comet:	1996 CE (20 YL)
Hale-Bopp Comet:	1997 CE (1 YL)
Comet McNaught:	2007 CE (10 YL)
Comet Elenin:	2010 CE (3 YL)
Comet Lovejoy:	2011 CE (1 YL)
Comet Frequency: 63.27 Years	

148 BCE - 120°

The **120°** of **148 BCE** ends the **Age of Aries (Children of Israel)** and begins the **Age of Pisces (Christian Era)**. In **146 BCE** we have the end of the Punic wars between Carthage/Rome . In **138 BCE to 111 BCE** the Han wage a campaign against the Minuye as China begins to take shape as a nation. In **135 BCE** the start of the Roman Servile wars begin, in **133 BCE to 89 BCE** sees the Han/Xiongnu war, **122 BCE to 105 BCE** the Jugurthine war is waged, from **113 BCE to 101 BCE** the Cimbrian war is fought, in **111 BCE** has the Han/Nanyue war, the Gojoseon/Han war goes from **109 BCE to 108 BCE**, in **109 BCE** the Han campaign against Dian is fought. **91 BCE to 88 BCE** brings the Social wars to Rome, from **89 BCE to 85 BCE** the **1st** Mithridatic war rages, **88 BCE** sees the end of the Seleucid/Parthian wars, from **88 BCE to 87 BCE** sees Sullas **1st** civil war and Halley's Comet appears in 87 BCE as well, from **83 BCE to 82 BCE** has the **2nd** Mithridatic war, and **82 BCE to 81 BCE** sees Sulla's **2nd** civil war.

76 BCE - 119°

From **74 BCE to 63 BCE** the **3rd** Mithridatic war is fought, in **71 BCE** we have the end of the Roman Servile wars, Pompey's fights his Georgian campaign in **65 BCE**, in **63 BCE** Pompey captures the city storied of Jerusalem. In **60 BCE** a massive earthquake strikes Portugal & Galicia. Julius Caesar's Gallic wars are fought from **58 BCE to 50 BCE**, while **55 BCE to 54 BCE** sees Julius Caesar's invasion of Britain. From **53 BCE to 51 BCE** the Parthian war with Marcus Licinius Crassus is fought. In **49 BCE to 45 BCE** we have Caesar's civil war fought, while **44 BCE to 30 BCE** sees the Roman civil wars (Post Caesarian, Liberator's civil war, Sicilian revolt, Fulvia's civil war). In **44 BCE** the fabled **"Caesar's Comet'** also known as **C/-43K1** appears in the skies, as Egyptian records denote a **44 BCE** passover event of **2** months, **7** days, and **2** years of forest fires, dust, cold, drought, crop failure, famine, **500,000** casualties locally: "Caesar's Comet" From **40 BCE to 33 BCE** Anthony's Parthian war is waged, and **34 BCE to 22 BCE** has the Chinese war bring an end to the last war of the degree **22** years before we change to the Common Era, as Halley's Comet makes the final appearance of a comet in the **119°** in **12 BCE**. There seems to be a palpable silence historically leading up the change in dating from "Before Common Era" to " the "Common Era." It has always been taught that the lands were rife with strife and insurgency, but all we have is silence!

*No noted wars 22 years before the noted time of Jesus Christ (JC) 22 BCE to 0 CE

4 BCE - 118°

And the first war is 43 years after the CE Common Era for a total of 65 years free of documented wars

We open the **118°** point in **17 CE** with a massive earthquake in Asia Minor region of Lydia. From **43 CE** to **96 CE** we have the Roman conquest of Britain. Around **50 CE** we have **Christianity** being founded. From **58 CE** to **63 CE** we have the Roman Parthian war, then in **60 CE** to **61 CE** Boudica's uprising, in **62 CE** in Naples and Pompeii a massive earthquake strikes the region, and from **66 CE** to **73 CE** the **1st** Roman/Jewish war is fought.

68 CE - 117°

In **70 CE** the Jewish Temple is destroyed stone by stone by Titus and the Roman army. In **79 BCE** just **17** years after a massive earthquake, Mount Vesuvius Volcano erupts destroying Pompeii & Herculaneum freezing people in time. The **79 CE** the Taupo Volcano erupts in North Island New Zealand as there seems to be a common ink for the eruption of Vesuvius as well. We have massive earthquake events in **110 CE** in Yunnan China and **115 CE** in Antioch. In **101 CE** to **102 CE** we have the **1st** Dacian war, in **105 CE** to **106 CE** we get the **2nd** Dacian war, from **115 CE** to **117 CE** the Kitos war is fought, and from **132 CE** to **136 CE** we end with the Bar Kokhba Revolt.

140 CE - 116°

Ice core samples from **172 CE** from the EPICA Dronning Maud Land shows an increase in volcanic sulphate that corresponds to the volcanic activity from the previous degree of **117**. From **161 CE to 166 CE** the Roman Parthian war is fought, from **166 CE to 180 CE** the Marcomannic wars rage, in **184 CE** to **205 CE** the Yellow Turban Rebellion is fought, **190 CE to 191 CE** sees the campaign against Dong Zhuo, and then in **194 CE to 199 CE** we have Sun Ce's conquest of Jiandong.

212 CE - 115°

In **225 CE** the Sub-Atlantic period of increased rainfall begins. **216 CE** sees Emperor Caracalla's Parthian war, in **225 CE** Zhuge Liang's Southern campaign is fought, from **228 CE to 234 CE** Zhuge Liang's Northern campaigns rages, from **247 CE to 262 CE** Jiang Wei's Northern campaigns are fought, in **263 CE** Wei's conquest of Shu occurs, and in **279 CE to 280 CE** Jin conquers Wu as China is the main theatre of war for the **115** degree.

284 CE - 114°

In **291 CE to 306 CE** we have the Eight Princes war, as in **300 CE** the New Madrid fault erupts with another massive earthquake. In **325 CE** the Council of Nicea formalizes the doctrines of the early church. We find in **350 CE** the oldest surviving Septuagint, and in **350 CE** it is believed the Talmud is written? From **376 CE to 382 CE** the Gothic war is fought.

356 CE - 113°

In **365 CE** in Crete Greece a massive earthquake strikes. The Nicene Christianity is named official religion of the Roman empire in **380 CE**. An earthquake event strikes Cape St. Vincent in **382 CE**. In **393 CE** the Synod of Hippo approves the early Christian canon. Egyptian records show a **416 CE** event with **1** year of dust, cold, famine, crop failure, drought, **250,000** local casualties. The eruption of Krakatau creates the Islands of Java & Sumatra as they are separated. The Egyptian event coincides with the eruption of Krakatau, as the effects were global. From **421 CE to 422** CE the Roman/Sasanian war closes out the degree.

* 416 CE - Krakatau erupts creating Java & Sumatra as Islands - One war noted 6 years after event - No wars until 72 years later

428 CE - 112°

30 - 495 CE: Roman rule ends, as the *Dark Ages* begin. The onset of the Early Dark Ages and the demise of the Roman Empire coincides with the eruption of Krakatau. This is a very silent **72** year period.

500 CE - 111°

We begin in **502 CE to 506 CE** with the Anastasian war, a massive earthquakes hits Antioch Turkey in **526 CE,** from **526 CE to 532 CE** we have the Iberian war, and the Iwai rebellion is **527 CE**. The Great Comet of **531 CE** appears in the skies. From **533 CE to 534 CE** we have the Vandalic war, **534 CE to 537 CE** has the war against the Moors, and from **534 CE to 554 CE** the Gothic war is waged. Egyptian records shows a **536 CE to 540 CE** event that coincides with the Dark Ages onset of **21** months of dust, diminished sunlight, dust, drought, cold, famine, crop failure, **2.9** million casualties globally. The Great Comet of **536 CE** comes **5** years after the previous Great Comet. Just **4** years later in **540 CE** we have a series of **3** comets that completely ushers in the Dark Ages. The Lazic war runs from **541 CE to 562 CE**, in **551 CE** in Beirut, Turkey, and Tripoli , there is a massive earthquake. In **570 CE** the Prophet Muhammad is born.

572 CE - 110°

The **110°** begins in **572 CE to 591 CE** Byzantine-Sasanian war, in **588 CE** the First Perso-Turkic war, in **598 CE to 614 CE** the Goguryeo-Sui wars, in **600 CE** the Frisnian-Frankish wars start , from **602 CE to 628 CE** the Byzantine-Sasanian war. In **610 CE** the Koran is written. In **619 CE** the Second Perso-Turkish war, **627 CE to 629 CE** the Third Perso-Turkish war is fought, in **627 CE to 630 CE** Taizong's campaign against Eastern Tujue, from **632 CE to 633 CE** the Ridda wars are fought, in **633 CE to 644 CE** the Muslim conquest of Persia occurs, in **634 CE** the start of Byzantine-Arab wars**.** In **639 CE** the Prophet Muhammad dies. In **640 CE to 657 CE** the Tang's wage a campaign against Western Turks, in **640 CE to 648 CE** Taizong's campaign against Xiyu states, and in **640 CE** the Tang campaign against Karakhoja.

644 CE - 109°

The Far East carries the action from **644 CE to 648 CE**, the Tang campaign against Karahasar, in **644 CE to 688 CE** Goguryeo-Tang war, from **645 CE to 646 CE** Taizong's campaign against Xueyantuo,   and from

648 CE the Tang campaign against Kucha is fought. In 650 CE we have the start of the Khazar-Arab wars. In 656 CE to 661 CE we have the First Fitna, in 657 CE the Tang conquest of Western Turks, from 670 CE to 676 CE the Silla-Tang wars in, 672 CE the Jinshin war, in 680 CE the start of Byzantine-Bulgarian wars. In 700 CE there is an eruption of Mt. Edziza, 711 CE to 718 CE the Umayyad conquest of Hispania, and from 715 CE to 718 CE the Frankish Civil War.

716 CE - 108°

*From 717 CE to 718 CE the Arab siege of Constantinople transpires, then in 732 CE the Battle of Tours is waged, in 735 CE to 737 CE Marwin ibn Muhammad invades Georgia, 749 CE has an earthquake event in the Levant Region, 751 CE has the Battle of Talas, in 755 CE to 763 CE the An Lushan Rebellion, in 758 CE the end of the Khazar-Arab wars, 772 CE has the start of the Saxon wars, and from 774 CE to 775 CE shows high Levels of **Carbon-14** in tree rings in Japan from a possible **gamma ray burst**.*

788 CE - 107°

In 793 CE the Frisnian-Frankish war ends, 804CE sees the end of the Saxon wars, 839 CE starts off the Bulgarian-Serbian wars. We have 3 major earthquakes within 9 years in the Mediterranean, Levant, and Near East. 847 CE Damascus Syria earthquake, 854 CE start of Croatian-Bulgarian wars, 856 CE Corinth Greece earthquake, and in 856 CE Qumis Iran earthquake event.

860 CE - 106°

The 106° sees in 869 CE to 883 CE the Zanj Rebellion transpire. The 106° point seems to be a continuation of the Earthquake swarm from the 107° of 847 CE to 856 CE, as 13 years later we pick back up with Earthquakes in 869 CE in Sendai Japan, 893 CE in Divin Armenia, in 893 CE in Ardabil Iran, and in 900 CE a New Madrid Earthquake. There were 4 major Earthquake events during the 31 year period (869 CE - 900 CE) for an average of 7.75 years, from 847 CE to 900 CE covering a 53 year period for a 7.57 per major Earthquake event.

932 CE - 105°

In 955 CE the Battle of Lechfield is fought, from 977 CE to 978 CE we have the War of the Three Henries, in 993 CE the First Goryeo-Khitan war, the 997 CE East Rongbuk Glacier Mt. Everest: a decrease in marine and increase in continental air masses since 1400, 999 CE ends the millenium with the Battle of Svolder, 1000 CE End of the Croatian-Bulgarian wars, in 1003 CE the end of the Bulgarian-Hungarian wars

1004 CE - 104°

We have from 1040 CE to 1080 CE the Oort minimum that brings about the Medieval Warm Period, 1042 CE in Baalbek, Palmyra, and Syria suffer a major Earthquake event, while the Great Comet of 1066 CE appears, a massive Earthquake strikes in 1068 CE in the Near East, in 1054 CE a Supernova creates the Crab Nebula, also in 1054 CE the church undergoes The Great Schism, in 1099 CE the Hodh Ech Chargui & Hodh El Gharbi regions of Mauritania become deserts, as the desertification of the planet continues, and in 1066 CE the Normans conquer England.

1076 CE - 103°

The 103° is fundamental in understanding the spread of Christianity/Catholicism over the next 600 plus years of human misery. The spread of one faith often causes the repression of others, and the Holy Crusades and Papal Wars brought this about.

All Catholic or Christian Holy Wars are in bold red from 103° (1076 CE) to the 94° (1580 CE)

In **1096 CE we begin with the First Holy Crusade**, in **1100 CE** to **1250 CE** we reach the Medieval maximum that brings about a Medieval Warm Period, in **1101 CE there is the Holy Crusade of 1101,** the Great Comet of **1106 CE** appears, in **1138 CE** in Aleppo Syria there is a major Earthquake. From **1145 CE to 1149 CE there is the Second Holy Crusade, and from 1147 CE to 1242 CE there is the Northern Holy Crusades.**

1148 CE - 102°

In **1157 CE** Hama Syria opens with a major Earthquake, in **1169 CE** in Sicily Italy Is struck with an Earthquake, in **1170 CE** the Eastern Meditteranean sees a major Earthquake, and in **1201 CE and 1202 CE** the Eastern Mediterranean is hit with two major Earthquakes. In the period from **1138 CE** to **1202 CE** there are **6** major Earthquakes that average **10.666** years in frequency. In **1169 CE to 1175 CE** the Norman Invasion of Ireland occurs, in **1180 CE** brings the end of the Byzantine-Arab wars. Religious Wars dominate the last portion of the **102°** as from **1189 CE to 1192 CE Third Holy Crusade is fought, in 1202 CE to 1204 CE** the **Fourth Holy Crusade,** in **1202 CE to 1214 CE** the **Anglo/French War,** from **1206 CE to 1337 CE** we have the Mongol Conquests, from **1208 CE to 1227 CE** the Livonian Holy Crusade is waged, and from **1213 CE to 1221 CE** we have the Fifth Holy Crusade.

1220 CE - 101°

Earthquakes begin the **101°** in **1222 CE** with a Cyprus Greece event, in **1268 CE** in Cilicia, Anatolia, and in **1290 CE** in Chihli China major earthquake. In **1228 CE** we get the **Sixth Holy Crusade,** from **1248 CE to** 1250 to 1850 - Little Ice Age **1254 CE Seventh Holy Crusade,** in **1270 CE** the **Eighth Holy Crusade,** from **1271 to 1272** the **Ninth Holy Crusade** is fought. We get the Great Comet of **1264 CE** right before we reach a cold spell in **1280 CE to 1350 CE** with the Wolf minimum.

1292 CE - 100°

In **1293 CE** in Kamakura Japan we have a volcanic event, and in **1303 CE** Crete Greece suffers a major earthquake. In **1320 CE** Pope John Paul XXII enacts witchcraft doctrines during a fearful period, as **1330 CE** brings an end of the Bulgarian-Serbian wars, and in **1337 CE** we have the start of **The Hundred Years War.** In **1345 CE** The Black Death/Bubonic Plague spreads across Europe killing over **100** million people. In **1348 CE** Friuli, Venice, and Rome suffer a massive earthquake, in **1355 CE** we see the end of the Byzantine-Bulgarian wars, and in **1356 CE** Basel Switzerland gets hit was a major earthquake.

1364 CE - 99°

From **1375 CE to 1378 CE** we get the *War of the Eight Saints,* in **1384 CE** Canterbury England suffers a major earthquake, in **1402 CE** we have a Great Comet appearance, from **1419 to 1434** we have the *Hussite Wars*, and in **1428 CE** Catalonia, Spain suffers an earthquake.

1436 CE - 98°

The period of 1450 CE to 1452 CE shows how volcanic activity and earthquakes, in conjunction with soar minimums can affect the climate, as in 1450 CE Aniakchak Volcano erupts, in 1450 CE Dasauopu Ice Core Nepal: chloride concentrations doubled, from 1450 CE to 1550 CE the Sporer minimum cold period runs, in 1452 CE Kuwae Volcano erupts, in 1450 CE the New Madrid Earthquake transpires again, and in 1453 CE the Kuwae Volcano erupts. This past period of 3 years suffered 3 volcanic eruptions and 1 major earthquake, for an average disaster occurring every 9 months. In **1453 CE** we have the end of *The Hundred Years War,* in 1453 CE we get the Fall of Constantinople, in **1467 CE** the *War of the Priests (really?)* is fought. In 1471 CE the Sakurajima Volcano erupts, in **1477 CE** the Bardarbunga Volcano erupts, in 1480 CE and 1482 CE Mount St. Helens Volcano erupts twice, as the average volcanic eruption is 2.75 years. From *1482 to 1484 - War of Ferrara* , and in 1484 CE Pope Innocent VIII begins European witch hunt, as the volcanic activity has cast a cold pall over the globe. In*1494 CE to 1498 CE the Italian War* rages, as the global magnetic field in **1500** sits just ≤11, and in **1500 CE** the Lewis Glacier - Microparticle Data bears clues to atmospheric anomalies.

1508 CE - 97°

In *1508 CE to 1516 CE we have the War of the League of Cambrai,* in **1509 CE** Istanbul Turkey sees a major earthquake event, from **1521 CE to 1526 CE** the *Italian War* rages, from **1527 CE to 1697** CE the Spanish Conquest of Yucatan is fought, from **1527 CE to 1528 CE** sees the *Hungarian Campaign*, **from 1530 CE to 1552 CE** we get the *Little War in Hungary*, from **1536 CE to 1538 CE** we have another *Italian War*, in **1531 CE** Lisbon Portugal sees a massive earthquake, in **1540 CE** Mount St. Helen Volcano erupts, **1542 CE to 1546 CE** we have a final *Italian War* , from **1545 CE to 1563 CE** the Council of Trent convenes to formalize church doctrine, the Great Comet of **1556 CE** appears, in **1556 CE** Shaanxi China has a major earthquake event, from **1551 CE to 1598 CE** *we get the French Wars of Religion* , in **1570 CE** Ferrara Italy suffers a massive earthquake, **1571 CE** has the Russo/Crimean War (**2014 also?**), in **1575 CE** in Valdivia Chile there is a major earthquake, the Great Comet of **1577 CE** appears in the records.

1580 CE - 96°

The **96°** of **1580 CE** sees **9** major disasters within the **72** year degree period, with an average major disaster rate of every **8** years. The Billy Mitchell Volcano erupts in **1580 CE** to start the degree off, in **1586 CE** the Kelut Volcano erupts, from **1592 CE to 1598 CE** we get the Japanese invasions of Korea, in **1593 CE** Raung Volcano erupts, in **1600 CE** the Huaynaputina Volcano erupts, and in **1601 CE** we get the coldest year in six centuries after Huaynaputina erupts in **1600 CE** causing famines globally, in **1604 CE** Arica Chile EQas a major earthquake event, in **1605 CE** in Shikoku & Honshu Japan there is a major earthquake, in **1605 CE** in Qiongshan& Hainan China there is a massive earthquake. In **1611 CE** we get *the release of the King James Bible during this period of upheaval. The **1650 CE** East Rongbuk Glacier **350** year trace element data, from **1635 CE to 1659 CE** we have the French/Spanish War. In **1639 CE** we have the First Bishops' War, in **1640 CE** the Second Bishops' War is fought, in **1640 CE** the Kamaga-Take Volcano erupts, in **1641 CE** Parker Volcano erupts, from **1641 CE to 1644 CE** the First War of Castro is fought, from **1644 CE to 1651 CE** we have the Scottish War of the Three Kingdoms, from **1645 CE to 1715 CE** we get the Maunder minimum cold period, in **1649 CE the Second War of Castro** is fought, and is the last openly Papal or Holy Wars, and in **1650 CE** the East Rongbuk Glacier **350** year trace atmospheric element data.*

1652 CE - 95°

*In **1660 CE** the Long Island Volcano erupts, in **1663 CE** the Usu Volcano erupts, then in **1663 CE** Quebec Canada there is a massive earthquake, in **1667 CE** Tarumai Volcano erupts, in **1667 CE** in Dubrovnik Croatia there is a large earthquake event, in **1667 CE** in Shamakhi Azerbaijan we get a large earthquake, in **1668 CE** Anatolia Turkey there is a large earthquake, in **1673 CE** the Gamkonora Volcano erupts, in **1680 CE** the Tongkoko Volcano erupts, then in **1680 CE** Krakatoa Volcano erupts with a massive eruption. The **95°** point is disaster central, as we have **6** volcanic eruptions and **4** major earthquakes within **20** years for an extremely high **2** year average. From **1683 CE to 1699 CE** the Great Turkish War is fought, **1683 CE to1684 CE** we have the War of the Reunions, in **1687 CE** Lima Peru suffers a major earthquake, in **1692 CE** in Salta Province Argentina there is a major earthquake, in **1692 CE** Port Royal Jamaica is hit with a major earthquake, in **1693 CE** in Catania Province Sicily we get a major earthquake, in **1694 CE** Irpinia Italy there is an earthquake. From **1701 CE to 1714 CE** we get the War of the Spanish Succession, **1703 CE** in Norcia Italy there is a major earthquake, in **1703 CE** in L'Aquil Italy there is a large earthquake, in**1703 CE** Kanto Japan suffers a major earthquake, in **1707 CE** and **1708 CE** the lands of Japan suffer several massive earthquakes, from **1718 CE to 1720 CE** the War of the Quadruple Alliance is waged. From**1687 CE to 1708 CE** we have **10** earthquakes for another high rate of **2.1** years per event.*

1724 CE - 94°

*In **1727 CE** in Tabriz Iran the earthquakes continue, in **1730 CE** Beijing China is struck with an earthquake, in **1730 CE** Kamchatka Russia suffers an earthquake, **1730 CE** see Valparaiso Chile get hit with an earthquake, as the Great Comet of **1744 CE** appears in the heavens, in **1746 CE** Lima and Callao Peru are struck with an earthquake, **1751 CE** sees Concepcion Chile hit with an earthquake. From **1727 CE to 1751 CE** there are **6** major earthquakes for a **6** year average. From **1754 CE to 1763 CE** the French/Indian War is fought, in **1755 CE** Northern Persia is hit with an earthquake, in **1755 CE** Boston Massachusetts there is a major earthquake, **1755 CE** Lisbon Portugal is struck with a major earthquake, in **1759 CE** the Eastern Mediterranean region is hit with a major earthquake, in **1762 CE** the Eastern Bay of Bengal is hit with a major earthquake event, in **1766 CE** St. Joseph, Trinidad, and Tobago are hit with an earthquake, in **1770 CE** Port Au-Prince Haiti is devastated by an earthquake, also in **1770 CE** India's Monsoons fail causing widespread famine, in **1773 CE** Guatemala is struck by an earthquake, from **1775 CE to 1783 CE** we have the American Revolutionary War, in **1780 CE** Iran suffers a major earthquake, **1783 CE** Calabria Italy is struck by an earthquake, in **1783 CE** Laki Volcano erupts, in **1786 CE** Sichuan China suffers a major earthquake, and in **1790 CE to 1820 CE** we reach the Daulton minimum cold period. There are **11*** *earthquakes and **1** volcanic eruption from **1755 BCE to 1786 BCE** for an average of **2.58** years per disaster event.*

1796 CE - 93°

*In **1797 CE** in Quito Ecuador and Cuzco Peru there is a massive earthquake, **1800 CE** sees San Diego hit with a major earthquake, in **1804 CE** the global population stands at **1** billion people. In **1810 CE** there is the U.S. Occupation of West Florida, from **1810 CE** to **1821 CE** we have the Mexican War of Independence, a Great Comet event happens in **1811 CE**, from **1812 CE** to **1815 CE** there is the War of **1812**, in **1815 CE** Tambora Volcano erupts causing **1816 CE** to be known as the " Year Without A Summer," after the eruption of Tambora in **1815**.In **1822 CE** the Galunggung Volcano erupts, the Great Comet of **1823 CE** shows, in**1825 CE** the Great Comet shows in the skies, in **1830 CE** the Mormons or Latter Day Saints are formed, **1833 CE** Sumatra in Indonesia is devastated with an earthquake, in **1835 CE** Cosiguina Volcano erupts, from **1835 CE** to **1836 CE** we get the Texas Revolution, in **1838 CE** the Mormon War is fought, from   **1839 CE** to **1842 CE** the First Opium War is waged, there is a Great Comet event in **1843 CE**, from **1846 CE** to **1848 CE** the Mexican/American War is waged, in **1854 CE** the Sheveluch Volcano erupts, from **1856 CE** to **1860 CE** the Second Opium War is fought, in **1858 CE** we have a Great Comet event, then in **1861 CE** there is a Great Comet sighting, from **1861 CE** to **1865 CE** the American Civil War rages. The period from **1796 CE** to **1868 CE** has only **3** major earthquakes and **4** volcanic events for an average of **10.285** years per.*

1868CE - 92°

*In **1868 CE** Arica Chile is struck with a major earthquake, **1875 CE** the Theosophical Society is founded by Madam Helena Blavatsky, **1875 CE** sees Askja Volcano erupt, in **1875 CE** Tarawera Volcano erupts, in **1882 CE** sees a Great Comet event, **1883 CE** has the legendary eruption of Krakatau Volcano, from **1899 CE** to **1901 CE** we have the famed Boxer Rebellion, **1900 CE** to present we have the Modern maximum, in **1900 CE** the Earth's global magnetic field level is ≤10, **1902 CE** sees the Santa Maria Volcano erupt, 1904 CE has Thelema founded, in **1906 CE** the San Francisco earthquake occurs, **1906 CE** also has a major earthquake event in Ecuador and Colombia, in **1907 CE** the Ksudach Volcano erupts, the period from **1868 CE to 1907 CE** has **5** volcanic eruptions and **3** major earthquakes for an average of **4.875** years per disaster event, **1910 CE** has the "Great Daylight Comet" event, **1910 CE** brings Halley's Comet back around, in **1911 CE** the Katmai Volcano erupts, in **1912 CE** the Negro Rebellion is fought, from **1914 CE** to **1919 CE** World War I is waged with the loss of tens of millions of lives, from **1917 CE** to **1923 CE** the Russian Civil War is fought, the Skjellerup-Maristany Comet appears in **1927 CE**, in **1927 CE** the global population is **2** billion people, **1930's CE** has the Rastafari movement, in the **1930's** the Nation of Islam is founded, In **1932 CE** the Cerro Azul Volcano erupts, from **1936 CE to 1939 CE** the Arab Revolt in Palestine transpires, from **1936 CE to 1939 CE** we have the Spanish Civil War, from **1939 CE to 1945 CE** World War II is fought with an estimated **75** million casualties. The period from **1908 CE to 1939** CE only sees **2** volcanic eruptions for an average disaster event period of **15.5** years.*

1940 CE - 91

This period sees the detonation of the first atomic bomb, the dropping of two atomic bombs on populated cities, and the eventual testing of over **2,500** thermonuclear devices in the air, below the sea, and below ground as well. The post war period of **1944 CE** to **1947 CE** sees the Jewish insurgency transpire in Palestine. From **1948 CE** to **1949 CE** has the Arab/Israeli War following the insurgency **1** year later. In **1950 CE** to **1953 CE** the Korean War controls the war headlines. A massive earthquake strikes in **1952 CE** in Kamchatka Russia, as Scientology is created by SciFi writer L. Ron Hubbard in **1952 CE** as well. From **1956 CE** to **1975 CE** has the French and the United States caught up in the Vietnam War. In **1956 CE** the Bezymianny Volcano erupts, and we have a Great Comet event in **1957 CE**. In **1960 CE** Valdivia Chile suffers a massive earthquake, the global population is 3 billion in **1960 CE**, in **1962 CE** we get the Seki-Lanes Comet, in **1964 CE** Prince William Sound suffers a massive earthquake, and in **1965 CE** Rat Island Alaska suffers a devastating earthquake. The Ikeya-Seski Comet appears in **1965 CE**. In **1966 CE** sees Anton Szandor LaVey starts the Church of Satan, **1967 CE** brings the Six Day War in the Middle East, in **1973 CE** the Raelian movement is founded. In **1973 CE** the Yom-Kippur War is waged, the global population rises to 4 billion people in **1974 CE**, the Comet West appears in **1976 CE**, from **1979 CE** to **1989 CE** the Soviet/Afghanistan War is fought, from **1980 CE** to **1988 CE** the Iran/Iraq War is waged, and in **1980 CE** Mount St. Helens Volcano erupts. The global population reaches 5 billion in **1987 CE**, **1990 CE** sees the Invasion of Kuwait, from **1990 CE** to **1991 CE** the Persian Gulf War is fought, from **1992 CE** to **1995 CE** the Bosnian War breaks out, and from **1996 CE** to **2001 CE** the Afghan Civil War is fought. Hyakutake Comet appears in **1996 CE**, and in **1997 CE** Comet Halle-Bopp appears and causes 39 members of the Heaven's Gate cult to commit suicide, in order to board a waiting UFO. In **1999 CE** the population rises to 6 billion, and in **2001 CE** to the present, the War in Afghanistan is fought, from **2003 CE** to **2011 CE** we have the Iraq War. In **2004 CE** Sumatra Indonesia is hit with a massive earthquake with a tsunami resulting. Comet McNaught appears in the skies in **2007 CE**, in **2007 CE** Operation Enduring Freedom occurs, in **2010 CE** Maule, Chile is struck by a massive earthquake, in **2010 CE** the Haiti earthquake devastates the small island nation, in **2010 CE** Chile is struck with another massive earthquake event, Comet Elenin appears in **2010 CE**, and Comet Lovejoy appears in the heavens in **2011 CE**.

2012 CE - 90°   9 (2012)   2011 - 7 billion people

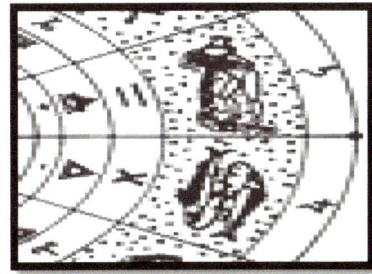  

Age of Pisces 120° to 90°   **Pisces symbol**   **Ruling planet is Jupiter & Cross**

240° to 210° Portion of the Heavens (10/12th)

90° to 60° 2012 CE to 4172 CE = 2160 years	Age of Aquarius to Age of Capricorn
Scientific Epoch:	?
Solfeggio Frequencies: 258 to 582	Varying range along the scale
Solfeggio Music Note:	
Volcanic Eruptions:	?
Earthquakes:	?
Geomagnetic Field:	?
Global Population:	?
Dendrochronology:	?
NOAA Ice Core:	?
Disasters:	?
Wars:	?
Rulership:	?
Religion:	?
Texts:	?
Diatonic G 432 Scale factor 9: 72°	72° solar point - 7200 days = 1 Katun 720° hexagon / tetrahedron sum Distance Earth to Moon = 2,592,000 miles / 360 = 7200
Geometry:	Hexagon and Hexahedron

Geometry: Hexagon and Hexahedron

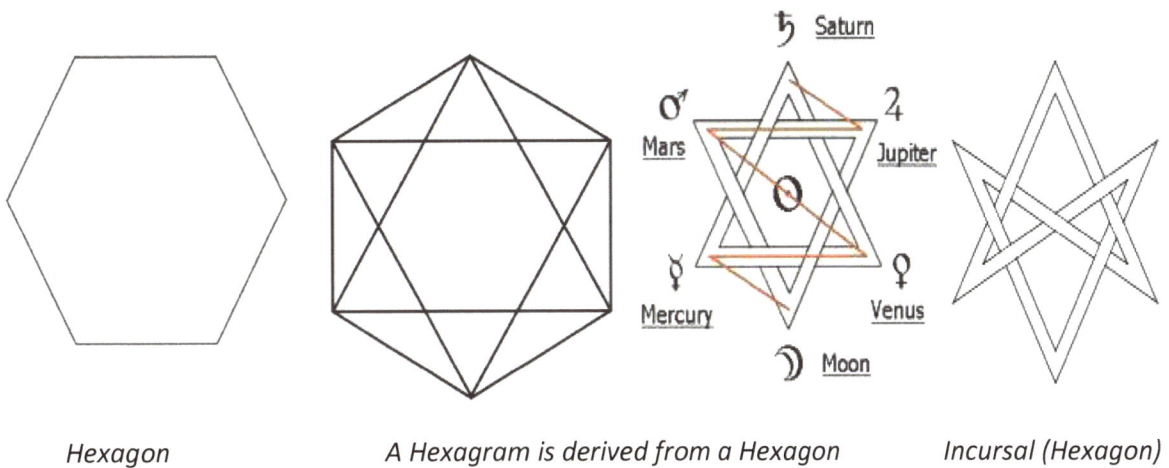

Hexagon   A Hexagram is derived from a Hexagon   Incursal (Hexagon)

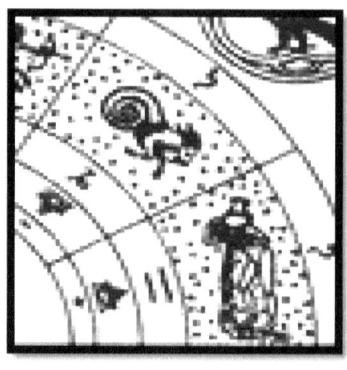  

Age of Aquarius 90° to 60° *Aquarius Water symbol* *Ruling planet is Saturn & Cross*

240° to 210° Portion of the Heavens (11/12th)

60° to 30° 4172 BCE to 6332 CE = 2160 years	Age of Capricorn to Age of Sagittarius
Scientific Epoch:	?
Solfeggio Frequencies:582 to 936/963	Varying range along the scale
Solfeggio Music Note:	G# and B
Volcanic Eruptions:	?
Earthquakes:	?
Geomagnetic Field:	?
Global Population:	?
Dendrochronology:	?
NOAA Ice Core:	?
Disasters:	?
Wars:	?
Rulership:	?
Religion:	?
Texts:	?
Diatonic G Scale factor 9: 36°	36° solar point - 3600 days = 1 Tun (Mayan) 360° solar point - 360° circle/square sum 3600° icosahedron sum - 3600 = 3600 X 10
Geometry:	Circle, Square, and Icosahedron

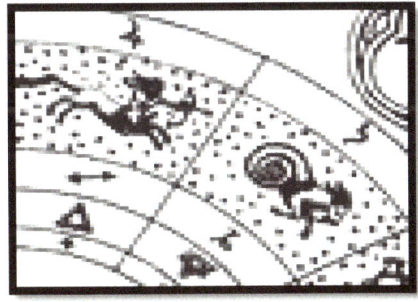  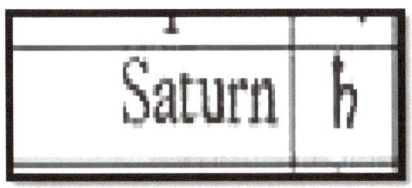

Age of Capricorn 60° to 30°   Capricorn Symbol   Ruling planet Saturn & Cross

240° to 210° Portion of the Heavens (12/12th)

30° to 360° 6332 CE to 8492 CE = 2160 years	Age of Sagittarius to Age of Scorpio
Scientific Epoch:	?
Solfeggio Frequencies: 936/963 to 258/285	Varying range along the scale
Solfeggio Music Note:	B and D#
Volcanic Eruptions:	?
Earthquakes:	?
Geomagnetic Field:	?
Global Population:	?
Dendrochronology:	?
NOAA Ice Core:	?
Disasters:	?
Wars:	?
Rulership:	?
Religion:	?
Texts:	?
Diatonic G Scale factor 9: None	
Geometry: none	
Astrology:	

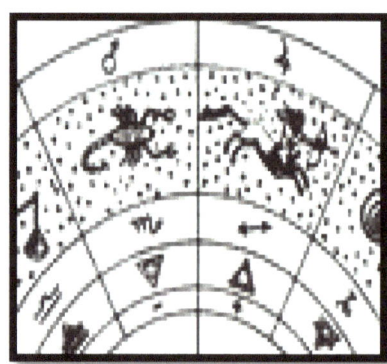  

Age of Sagittarius 30° to 360°   Sagittarius Symbol   Ruling planet Jupiter & Cross

Conclusions

The celestial and terrestrial records of events shows a dramatic gap of millions of years in information. The volcanic, earthquake, solar flares, comets, global magnetic field level, and other disaster events only show up in the recent geological record. The period before 10,000 BCE leaves millions of years before we find any volcanic or crustal evidence of disaster. Our modern system of detection has improved our understanding in recent years, and has helped our record keeping of these disasters has improved as well.

I feel that when the reader collates all of these events and findings, they will understand these events as our ancients intended. We are looking with modern eyes at ancient understanding! One must first use their terminology to see the correspondence. I will not tie all of the strings together for the reader, as the reader must be the seeker of true understanding. Understand our reality for yourself!

Various Graphs

Global Magnetic Field Level from 12,000 BCE to 2010 CE

												12
									* *	*	*		11
											*		10
									*		*		9
*			*	*		*		*					8
		*			*		*						7
												6
												5
												4
												3
												2
												1
												0
10,000 BCE	9000 BCE	8000 BCE	7000 BCE	6000 BCE	5000 BCE	4000 BCE	3000 BCE	2000 BCE	1000 BCE	1000 CE	2000 CE	

Major Volcanic Eruptions from 12,000 BCE to 2010 CE

												60
												55
												50
												45
											*	40
												35
												30
									*			25
												20
												15
										*		10
					*	*						5
	*	*	*	*			*	*				0
10,000 BCE	9000 BCE	8000 BCE	7000 BCE	6000 BCE	5000 BCE	4000 BCE	3000 BCE	2000 BCE	1000 BCE	1000 CE	2000 CE	

Major Earthquakes from 12,000 BCE to 2010 CE

	10,000 BCE	9000 BCE	8000 BCE	7000 BCE	6000 BCE	5000 BCE	4000 BCE	3000 BCE	2000 BCE	1000 BCE	1000 CE	2000 CE	
												*	80
													75
													70
													65
													60
													55
													50
													45
													40
													35
													30
													25
													20
											*		15
													10
													5
									*	*			0

Wars & Major Conflicts from 5000 BCE to 2010 CE

	10,000 BCE	9000 BCE	8000 BCE	7000 BCE	6000 BCE	5000 BCE	4000 BCE	3000 BCE	2000 BCE	1000 BCE	1000 CE	2000 CE	
													90
													85
										*		*	80
											*		75
													70
													65
													60
													55
													50
													45
													40
													35
									*				30
													25
													20
									*				15
													10
													5
													0

Disasters Pauses Warfare!

Event	Date	Global Magnetic Field Level	Last War Pre-disaster	First War Post Disaster	Total Period No Wars	Notable
Great Flood	2344 BCE	≥8	2492 BCE	2295 BCE	197 years	Black Sea becomes a salt sea
Sodom & Gomorrah	2184 BCE	≥8	2271 BCE	2150 BCE 2125 BCE Solar Max	121 years	Dead Sea created and 5 cities destroyed
Exodus Disaster	1487 BCE - 1447 BCE	9 (+1)	1507 BCE	1457 BCE 1390 BCE Solar Min	50 years	Preceded by Dwarka and Santorini disasters in 1500 BCE
Babylonian Exile	580 BCE to 510 BCE	11 (+2)	650 BCE 565 BCE Solar Max	430 BCE	150 years	Forced evacuation?
Time of Christ	2 BCE to 30 CE?	11	22 BCE	43 BCE	65 years	No wars before or after the time of Christ?
Krakatoa Volcano	416 CE	≤11 (-.5)	422 BCE (6 YL)	494 CE	72 years (78 years total)	Massive eruption brings on the early Dark Ages
Curious						
Degraded Earth	2295 BCE	≥8	2492 BCE	2150 BCE	145 years	First desert appears in Egypt in 2300 BCE
Philistines Rise	1200 BCE	9	1225 BCE	1046 BCE 1080 BCE Solar Max	154 years	Fall of Troy, Myceneans, and the Hittites
David & Solomon?	1000 BCE	11	1046 BCE	740 BCE 770 BCE Solar Min	260 years	Egyptian Upheaval Period

Great Flood Global Event 2344 BCE

Categories	Date	Last Pre-Event	First Post Event	Date	Total
War	2492 BCE	Nimrod-Halik War	Lugal-zage-si wars	2295 BCE	193 YL
Earthquake	2350 BCE	New Madrid	Xia China	1831 BCE	519 YL
Volcano	2420 BCE	Mt. Vesuvius	Long Island Volcano Changbaishan Volcano Liamuiga Volcano Pago Volcano	2020 BCE	400 YL
Global Magnetic Field	2452 BCE	≥8	≥8	N/A	
Solar Minimum	2860 BCE			1390 BCE	1470 YL
Solar Maximum	3100 BCE			2125 BCE	975 YL
Global Population	2344 BCE	20 million	27 million	2300 BCE	+7M

Passover Event of 2184 BCE

Categories	Date	Last Pre-Event	First Post Event	Date	Total
War	2295 BCE	Lugal-zage-si	Glutian attacks Akkad	2150 BCE	145 YL
Earthquake	2350 BCE	New Madrid	Xia, China	1831 BCE	519 YL
Volcano	2420 BCE	Mt. Vesuvius	Long Island Volcano Changbaishan Volcano Liamuiga Volcano Pago Volcano	2020 BCE	275 YL
Global Magnetic Field	2184 BCE	≥8	≥8	2184 BCE	Even
Solar Minimum	2860 BCE			1390 BCE	1470 YL
Solar Maximum	3100 BCE			2125 BCE	975 YL
Global Population	2184 BCE	27 million	27 million	2184 BCE	Even

Exodus Passover Event 1487 BCE

Categories	Date	Last Pre-Event	First Post Event	Date	Total
War	1507 BCE	Kassites war	Har-Meggido Battle	1457 BCE	50 YL
Earthquake	1831 BCE	Xia, China	Sparta, Greece	464 BCE	1367 YL
Volcano	1500 BCE	Avachinsky	Taupo	1460 BCE	50 YL
Global Magnetic Field	1487 BCE	9	9	1487 BCE	Up 1
Solar Minimum	2860 BCE			1390 BCE	1470 YL
Solar Maximum	3100 BCE			2125 BCE	975 YL
Global Population	1487 BCE	50 million	50 million	1487 BCE	+23M

Exile Passover Events 580 BCE

Categories	Date	Last Pre-Event	First Post Event	Date	Total
War	650 BCE	Lelantine war	Persian/Greek wars	499 BCE	151 YL
Earthquake	1831 BCE	Xia, China	Sparta, Greece	464 BCE	1367 YL
Volcano	1050 BCE	Mt. Pinatubo	Tongariro	550 BCE	500 YL
Global Magnetic Field	580 BCE	11	11	580 BCE	*Up 2*
Solar Minimum	770 BCE			360 BCE	410 YL
Solar Maximum	1085 BCE			565 BCE	520 YL
Global Population	580 BCE	50 million	50 million	580 BCE	Even

Christian Era Passover Event 0 CE

Categories	Date	Last Pre-Event	First Post Event	Date	Total
War	22 BCE	Chinese war	Roman conquest of Britain	43 CE	65 YL
Earthquake	60 BCE	Portugal & Galicia	Lydia & Asia Minor	17 CE	77 YL
Volcano	50 BCE	Apoyeque & Ambrym	Vesuvius & Taupo	79 CE	129 YL
Global Magnetic Field	0 CE	11	11	0 CE	
Solar Minimum	360 BCE			540 CE	700 YL
Solar Maximum	340 BCE			1090 CE	1430 YL
Global Population	0 CE	100 million	100 million	0 CE	*+50M*

Major Volcanic Events & Solar Minimums & Maximums

Solar Minimum	Major Eruptions	Major Eruptions	Solar Maximum
9170 BCE		8750 BCE	8695 BCE
8220 BCE	8230 BCE, 8130 BCE		7870 BCE
7520 BCE	7560 BCE, 7480 BCE, 7460 BCE	7420 BCE	7415 BCE
7310 BCE			7175 BCE
7040 BCE	6940 BCE		6720 BCE
6400 BCE	6440 BCE		6310 BCE
6220 BCE	6200 BCE	6060 BCE, 6050 BCE	6105 BCE
5990 BCE	5980 BCE		5850 BCE
5710 BCE	5700 BCE	5677 BCE	5665 BCE
5620 BCE	5560 BCE, 5550 BCE X 2		5440 BCE
5260 BCE	5250 BCE	4750 BCE, 4360 BCE, 4350 BCE, 4340 BCE	4600 BCE
3940 BCE	4050 BCE, 4000 BCE		3785 BCE
3630 BCE		3580 BCE X 2, 3550 BCE	3565 BCE
3500 BCE			3420 BCE
3340 BCE		3200 BCE	3100 BCE
2860 BCE	2420 BCE	2020 BCE X 2, 1900 BCE, 1890 BCE, 1860 BCE	2125 BCE
1390 BCE	1750 BCE, 1645 BCE, 1610 BCE, 1500 BCE, 1460 BCE, 1370 BCE	1050 BCE	1085 BCE
770 BCE		550 BCE	565 BCE
360 BCE	400 BCE	250 BCE, 100 BCE, 50 BCE X 2, 79 CE, 230 CE, 240 CE, 416 CE, 450 CE, 540 CE, 700 CE, 710 CE	340 CE
1040 CE - 1080 CE Oort Minimum Medieval Warm Period	800 CE, 930 CE, 934 CE, 969 CE		1090 CE
1100 CE - 1250 CE Medieval Max	1258 CE		1265 CE
1280 CE - 1350 CE Wolf Minimum	1280 CE		1400 CE
1450 CE - 1550 CE Sporer Minimum	1450 CE, 1452 CE, 1471 CE, 1477 CE, 1480 CE, 1482 CE, 1540 CE, 1580 CE	1586 CE, 1593 CE, 1600 CE	1602 CE
1645 CE - 1715 CE Maunder Minimum	1640 CE, 1641 CE, 1660 CE, 1663 CE, 1667 CE, 1673 CE, 1680 CE X 2	1739 CE, 1755 CE	1753 CE
1790 CE - 1820 CE Daulton Minimum	1783 CE, 1815 CE, 1822 CE, 1835 CE	1854 CE, 1875 CE	1860 CE

1900 - Present Modern Max	1875 CE, 1883 CE, 1902 CE, 1907 CE, 1911 CE, 1932 CE, 1956 CE, 1980 CE, 1991 CE		

Science has shown a very close relationship between volcanic activity and solar flares. This chart shows the eruption events during the solar minimums and the solar maximums.

"The Birth of Venus & Kiloyear Events"

Date	Event	YL = Years Later	Result
13,000 BCE	Birth of Venus?		Legend has Venus born of Jupiter @ this time
13,000 BCE	Older Dryas ends		Ice Age ends with the birth of Venus the comet/planet
12,700 BCE	Bolling-Allerod Oscillation	300 YL	An extremely warm oscillation period
12,670 BCE	Holocene epoch starts	30 YL	The period that we exist in today
12,263 BCE	Unusual warm period	407 YL	The global temperature increases mysteriously
11,700 BCE	Allerod Oscillation	563 YL	The Allerod warm oscillation causes sea levels to rise a catastrophic 65'7"
11,000 BCE	Massive extinction	700 YL	Holocene extinction features a northern latitude passover with the mass extinction of woolly mammoth, saber tooth tigers, and megafauna
10,900 BCE	Impact event?	100 YL	Possible impact date from ice core samples
10,800 BCE	Global temperature drop of 27° F	100 YL	Global temperatures plummet 27° F within 200 years of the massive extinction
10,000 BCE	World sea levels	800 YL	Seal levels rise around the world without the aid of floods
9500 BCE	Warm period	500 YL	Plato's destruction of Atlantis during an extremely warm period
7400 BCE	9.4 Kiloyear Event	2100 YL	Impact event
7000 BCE	Preboreal ends	400 YL	Boreal period begins
6200 BCE	8.2 Kiloyear Event	800 YL	Global temperatures suddenly drops 1° to 11° F
5620 BCE	**Thermal Maximum**	580 YL	Planetary temperatures reach the highest point in **125,000** years after temperatures drop up to **11° F** curiously, as this shows external forces cause true global warming versus the footprints of an industrialized mankind
5620 BCE	**Solar Minimum?** - How do we reach the hottest temperatures in a 125,000 years while starting a solar minimum period for flares?		
5000 BCE	Older Peron Transgression starts	620 YL	This warm period follows the thermal maximum
4000 BCE	Older Peron Transgression ends	1000 YL	Warm period ends

3940 BCE	Solar minimum		
3900 BCE	5.9 Kiloyear Event	100 YL	Impact event
2350 BCE	First noted earthquake	1550 YL	First noted earthquake in millions of years
2344 BCE	Global Flood Event	6 YL	Global Flood Event
2300 BCE	First deserts	44 YL	The 1st deserts on earth appear in Egypt as a result of the 2344 BCE passover
2200 BCE	4.2 Kiloyear Event	100 YL	Impact Event
2184 BCE	Sodom & Gomorrah Event	16 YL	Planetary passover event that destroys the 5 cities of the Dead Sea valley
1487 BCE	Exodus Passover Event	697 YL	Passover disasters noted in Egyptian and Biblical records
800 BCE 770 BCE	2.8 Kiloyear Event Solar minimum	687 YL	Greece & Rome rise from the impact event as Israel & Judah fall during this time, and will lead to the eventual forced relocation of the Hebrews to Babylon
600 CE	1.4 Kiloyear Event	1400 YL	Impact Event continues the Dark Ages
1500 CE	0.5 Kiloyear Event	900 YL	Impact Event

Legend has Venus being borne of Jupiter at some point in time. These legends have not been proven in their entirety, but have yet to be disproven! Immanuel Velikosky was the most noted proponent of this platform, and I decided to look at all of the different information available to us today. This cross reference of NOAA Ice Cores, Earthquakes, Volcanoes, Wars, Solar Minima and Maxima, Kiloyear Events, and much more. This scientific basis opened my eyes to how the legends began to mesh with a possible real event.

Venus was possibly born in 13,000 BCE, as the Older Dryas Ice Age comes to a sudden end, as the Bolling-Allerod Oscillation begins in 12,700 BCE with an unusually warm period, and this ushers in the Holocene epoch in 12,670 BCE, which is the era that we live in today. The Allerod warm oscillation causes sea levels to rise a catastrophic 65'7" in 11,700 BCE. The Holocene extinction features a northern latitude passover with the mass extinction of woolly mammoth, saber tooth tigers, and megafauna, in 11,000 BCE with no known internal or external cause. NOAA ice core samples show a possible impact date of 10,900 BCE. The global temperatures plummet 27° F in 10,800 BCE. In 10,000 BCE global sea levels rise without the fingerprint of humanity.

Plato's destruction of Atlantis in 9500 BCE is given more credence as we now know that sea levels rose extremely during this era. We have our Kiloyear Event in 7400 BCE with the 9.4 Event as a possible disaster from the skies. The Preboreal ends in 7000 BCE, as the Boreal period begins. The global *temperatures suddenly drops 1°F to 11° F in 6200 BCE with the 8.2 Kiloyear Event. We reach a thermal maximum in 5620 BCE with the highest temperatures in 125,000 years, as we reach a solar minimum for Sun spots in the same year as we reach a thermal maximum. What is the force that caused this extreme temperature spike when we were in a solar minimum?*

The Older Peron Transgression begins in 5000 BCE, and this warm period ends as swiftly as it began in 4000 BCE. In 3900 BCE we get the 5.9 Kiloyear impact event. We get the first noted earthquake in millions of year in 2350 BCE. This is a big clue to the prior positive integrity of the earth before the egg was broken, as earthquakes only occur because the egg was broken in 2344 BCE. The 4.2 Kiloyear Event in 2200 BCE brings more decimation from the heavens. In 2184 BCE we get the destruction that was related Biblically as the disasters of Sodom, Gomorrah, Bela/Zoar, Zeboim, and Admah.

In 1487 BCE we get the disasters noted in the Egyptian records, and Biblically as the Exodus Passover tale. In 800 BCE we get the 2.8 Kiloyear Impact Event, as the empires of Greece and Rome rise from the impact event as Israel and Judah fall during this time, and this will lead to the eventual forced relocation of the Hebrews to Babylon. In 400 CE we get the 1.4 Kiloyear Event that ushers in the Dark Ages, and we get the final Kiloyear event on record in 1500 CE with the 0.5 Event.

Our inner planets may have been affected by the parabolic trajectory that Venus assumed during the early years of her birth. NASA imaging has recently shown that when the solar winds die down, after 45 minutes Venus begins to assume the shape of a comet with tail. Venus is the only known planet that appears as a comet. Here's a thought! What is the solar winds died down for 45 hours, days, or weeks. Would Venus take flight from her celestial bar?